SAS AND ELITE FORCES GUIDE
MENTAL
ENDURANCE

SAS AND ELITE FORCES GUIDE
MENTAL
ENDURANCE

HOW TO DEVELOP MENTAL TOUGHNESS
FROM THE WORLD'S ELITE FORCES

CHRIS McNAB

LYONS PRESS
Guilford, Connecticut

An imprint of Globe Pequot Press

To buy books in quantity for corporate use
or incentives, call **(800) 962-0973**
or e-mail **premiums@GlobePequot.com**.

Lyons Press is an imprint of Globe Pequot Press.

Library of Congress Cataloging-in-Publication Data is available on file.

ISBN: 978-0-7627-8785-2

Project Editor: Michael Spilling
Design: Brian Rust
Illustrations: Tony Randell

Printed in Italy

10 9 8 7 6 5 4 3 2 1

CONTENTS

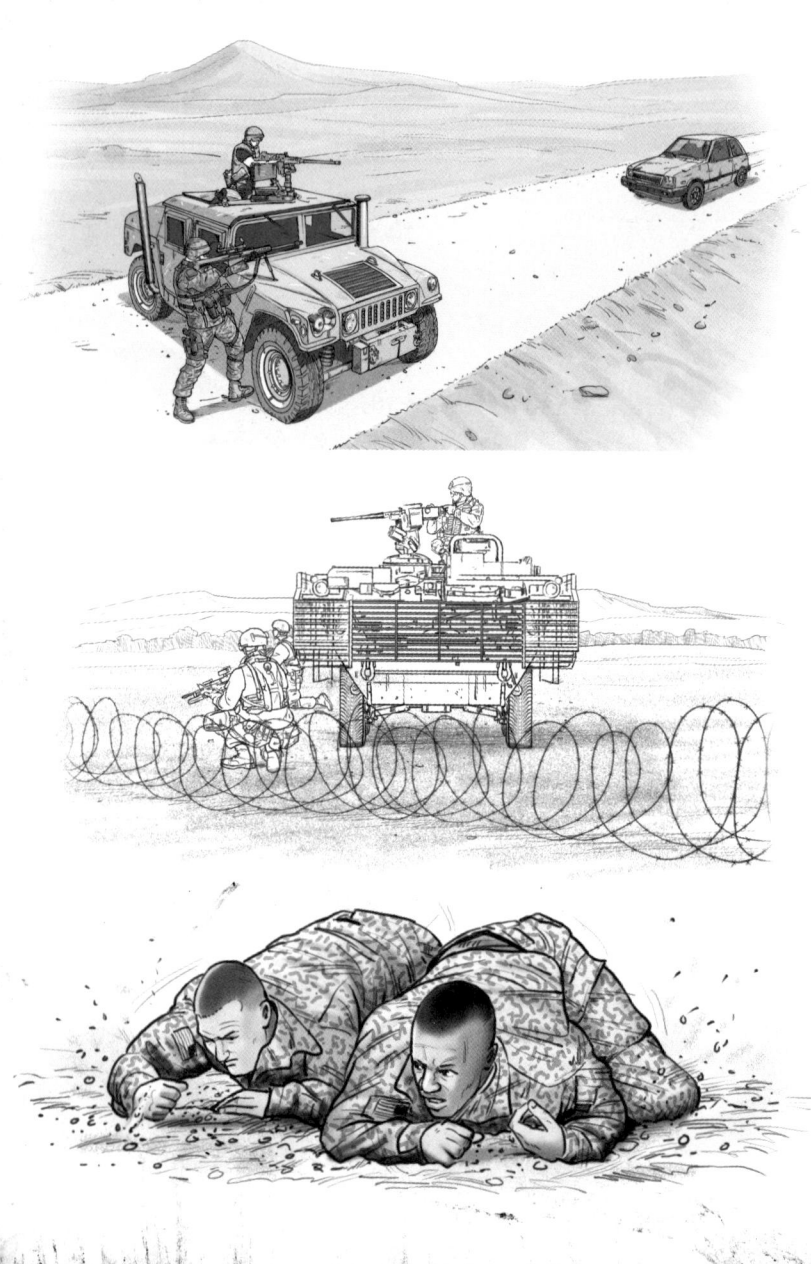

When men and women are recruited into the armed services, they enter a profession unlike any other, with the very real prospect that one day they might experience the violence and chaos of combat. From the outset, therefore, they have to exhibit mental toughness, self-discipline and a warrior spirit.

> 'You've never lived until you've almost died. For those who fight for it, life has a meaning the protected will never know.'

This now-famous quotation was a popular saying in the Studies and Operations Group (SOG), the Special Forces units that operated deep within enemy territory during the Vietnam War. In many ways it encapsulates the profound distinction between civilian and military life. In the civilian world, the greatest mental challenges tend to come from the realms of work, money, health and family. Violence, by contrast, is generally an incidental and irregular occurrence, and one that can often be avoided by the

• •

From keeping the peace in active war zones to escaping enemy fire, military service requires a mental toughness that enables soldiers to perform at their best under all circumstances.

1

Above all, soldiers, sailors, airmen and marines need to possess mental endurance if they are to survive the experience of military service.

What It Takes

Warrior Spirit

Combat is an intense experience both psychologically and physically. Here a soldier survives the blast of a nearby artillery explosion; exposure to prolonged shellfire has historically been a leading cause of post-traumatic stress disorder, even amongst elite troops.

simplest of safety precautions. (There are of course some troubled parts of the world that are unfortunate exceptions to this rule.)

For the soldier, airman, marine or sailor, however, violence can be encountered – indeed, sought out – on a scale or intensity that is almost unimaginable to any civilian who has not lived through a war itself. The experiences of combat present sights, sounds and sensations of unique force – bullets splitting the air with a supersonic crack; explosions

Security Duties

A US Army patrol performs routine security duties at a checkpoint in Iraq. The psychological challenge for the men is to remain vigilant for long periods under sustained levels of threat, with each soldier taking responsibility for a particular aspect or sector of group protection.

Comradeship

Military service deliberately promotes comradeship and a sense of belonging. Shared experiences can unite individuals and improve unit cohesion under fire.

demolishing entire buildings with a single enormous blast; directing devastating air strikes with just a GPS designator and a radio; mutilations of almost fantastic horror; the violent deaths of friends, sometimes in large numbers; the misery of observing civilian families caught in the crossfire; the shock of killing another human being. Such experiences cannot but have a powerful effect on the human psyche.

Yet even in peacetime, the demands of military service are quite distinct. Soldiers have to endure hard training regimes, some of which would test professional athletes to their limits. They have to comply with harsh discipline, curtailed sleep, an often-unimaginative diet and a culture with a generally intolerant attitude towards weakness. They also have to be organized, smart and respectful of authority, articulate in communication and able to perform their duties with efficiency and intelligence.

Making the Grade

We expect a lot of those we put in uniform, and not everyone is cut out for this service. Typical failure rates for those attempting to pass basic training in a regular infantry regiment can be in the region of 20–30 per cent. If we look at those who attempt to join the Special Forces, such as

Basic Training

Basic training aims to prepare recruits for military life by combining physical and mental trials. On route marches such as these, the soldier needs mentally to 'compartmentalize' the discomforts of heavy loads and focus on the job in hand.

the Special Air Service (SAS) or US Navy SEALs, then the failure rates spiral upwards to the region of 75–90 per cent. Physical limitations are often a cause of drop-outs, but a significant proportion are sent home or back to their original units because they didn't quite exhibit the right mental requirements.

In mass conscript armies, such as those recruited during the world wars or in many of the pre-20th-century conflicts, the psychological profile of the individual soldier was not necessarily an impediment to joining up – during moments of genuine national crisis, every man who can be put into the field is of use. In modern professional armies, by contrast, selectivity can be put into play. Those who attempt to join the military must exhibit, or come to exhibit during training, a mixture of qualities that can be roughly compiled under the umbrella heading of 'character'. The definition of character has been penned by many military theorists. Napoleon once said, with characteristic fire: 'True character always pierces through in moments of crisis… There are sleepers whose awakening is terrifying.' The great strategic thinker Carl von Clausewitz was slightly more nuanced:

> We repeat again: strength of character does not consist solely in having powerful feelings, but in maintaining one's balance in spite of them. Even with the violence of emotion, judgement and principle must still function like a ship's compass, which records the slightest variations however rough the sea.
> – Clausewitz, *On War*, 1.3

Clausewitz gives a more useful definition of character, being that of an individual who can balance strong emotions with intelligence and judgement. Such a mental balancing act is particularly relevant to modern soldiers, who might find themselves shifting between the roles of combat soldier and peacekeeper several times within the space of a single day. What emerges here is a moral quality, and British Army General Sir James Glover stated this principle of character with a perfect clarity:

> A man of character in peace is a man of courage in war. Character is a habit. The daily choice of right and wrong. It is a moral quality which grows to maturity in peace and is not suddenly developed in war. The conflict between morality and necessity is eternal. But at the end of the day the soldier's moral dilemma is only resolved if he remains true to himself.
> – Glover, *A Soldier and His Conscience*, 1983

The notion of character being a 'habit' is important for soldiers, as it implies consistency. In turn, consistency implies reliability, and a soldier who has a reliable inner strength is one on whom other men can depend in combat. Furthermore, Glover points to the fact that being a soldier is, in many ways, a profession that demands a high level of moral rigour – failures in those moral standards can lead to atrocity, indiscipline and often defeat.

Team Support

Being able to depend on team members in times of crisis is vital for the completion of successful missions. Each team member will contribute a military specialty, be it marksman, engineer or platoon leader, and the team's efficiency depends on each soldier mastering his particular skill.

Under Pressure

These US soldiers have a matter of seconds to ascertain whether a situation is about to become deadly. They must make behavioural and tactical judgements, within the set rules of engagement, about whether it is justifiable to open fire on the vehicle.

This book is about the character of the modern soldier. More specifically, it is about the mental qualities that soldiers should have, and how they can be acquired if they are not there in the first place. The emphasis on mental endurance, rather than physical strength or tactical awareness, is critical. The demands placed upon soldiers can be so extreme that if not managed properly they can lead to a lifetime of mental disability, ranging from depression to the draining effects of post-traumatic stress disorder (PTSD). If the soldier is in control of his faculties, intelligence and emotions, however, he can be an individual force to be reckoned with on the battlefield.

That said, some cautions are in order. The author is not a serving soldier, although his profession brings him into regular contact with those in the military. To give weight to the discussions to come, therefore, the theories are based directly on those espoused by military psychologists and by commanders in the field. Other input comes from soldiers who have actually tasted combat, and who know the difference between what makes a soldier crack or excel. Ultimately, this book is written with a deep respect for those who will, as part of their profession, risk the ultimate price for their service to the country.

In a diet-conscious age, many people are aware of the recommended daily calorie intake of 2500 calories (kcal) for an average adult male and 1800–2000 calories for an average adult female. Factors such as age, size and lifestyle affect this amount – if you are very sedentary, for example, you should either decrease your calorie intake or take more exercise. Equally, if you are doing significantly more than the 150 minutes of physical activity a week that is recommended by US and UK government guidelines, your diet should take into account the extra number of calories you will burn off.

For military personnel, the situation is far more extreme. The soldier's career is inherently physically demanding – military personnel can consume up to twice the recommended daily calorie intake, depending on their lifestyle, environment and physique. During the 40-plus week training programme for the Royal Marines, for example, recruits consume an average of 4000 calories a day, yet still manage to lose weight, such is the energy consumption. Studies show that

....

The importance of nutrition and rest to soldiers cannot be overemphasized if they are to stay at the peak of their mental endurance throughout challenging situations.

2

No matter how fit a soldier feels himself to be, without adequate nutrition he will soon run low on energy, both mental and physical.

Diet, Nutrition and Rest

Cooking in the Field

No matter how basic the facilities, servicemen should always aim to eat a proper meal taken from a variety of food groups, containing enough calories to sustain them.

soldiers on combat operations burn about 4000 calories a day. For a soldier, therefore, diet is critical – and not just for physical stamina. Poor diet can add to a range of mental issues, including fatigue, confusion, mood changes and a deficient concentration. All these problems can have critical implications on a battlefield.

Varied Diet

Your daily allowance of calories should come from a variety of food groups, the main categories of which are:

- carbohydrates
- proteins
- fats (together known as macronutrients)
- micronutrients (vitamins and minerals)

Carbohydrates

Carbohydrates are the main source of energy for the body and are vital for a soldier's ability to endure exercise, combat missions and other physical demands. They are made up of four main groups:

- **monosaccharides**, the most basic type of carbohydrates in the form of simple sugars such as glucose or fructose;
- **disaccharides**, a sugar compound of two monosaccharides, such as sucrose or lactose;
- **oligosaccharides**, which contain two to 10 components and are found in many vegetables;
- **polysaccharides**, the most complex type of carbohydrate found in many cereals.

In terms of what we eat, simple carbohydrates form most of the sugars in our diet, while complex carbohydrates form the bulk of starchy foods, such as bread, pasta and cereals, plus many fruit and vegetables. Simple carbohydrates or sugars such as glucose provide the body with almost instant energy, which is why glucose is used in sports drinks.

A diet low in carbohydrates will not necessarily be dangerous, as the body also uses proteins and fats to provide energy, but carbohydrates are very important for the active lifestyle of a military career. Not enough carbohydrates in your diet can cause fatigue and weight loss, the latter as the body burns off stored fat instead of the energy derived from the carbohydrates. The recommended daily intake of carbohydrates is 45–65 per cent of your daily calorie consumption.

Proteins

Proteins are made up of polypeptides, which are strings of amino acids containing nitrogen. During digestion, these strings are broken down and metabolized by the body. Proteins are indispensable nutrients, as the body cannot make these essential

Food Types

This digram shows the breakdown of foods that should be eaten over the day, including meat or fish, dairy, fruit and vegetables, and starchy foods. Depending on your physical and mental training needs, you might want to consume larger amounts of carbohydrates to ensure that you have adequate supplies of energy to sustain you.

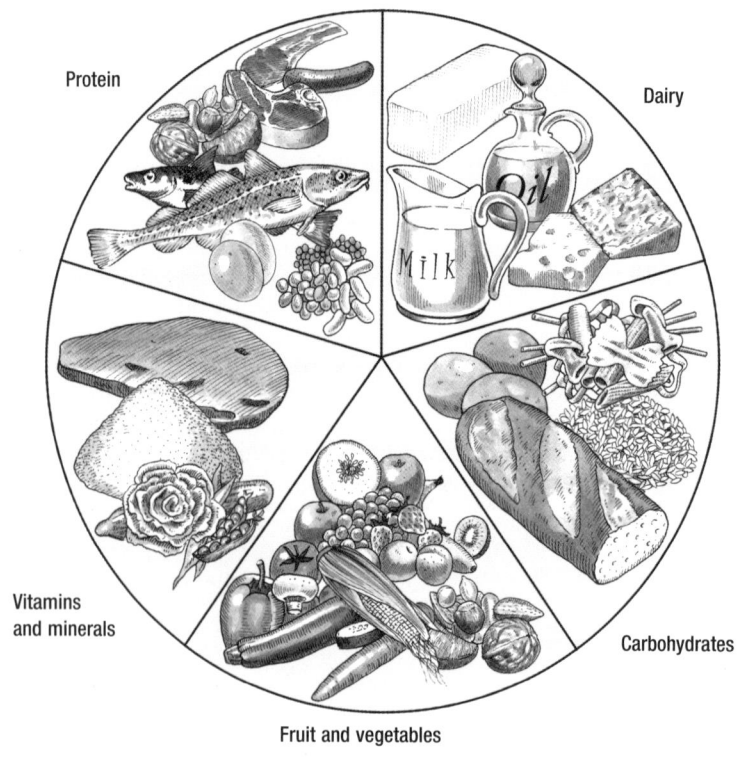

Protein

Dairy

Vitamins and minerals

Carbohydrates

Fruit and vegetables

amino acids and must obtain them from foods. They are primarily used for the growth and repair of the body, including cellular processes and muscle, skin, bone and blood production and health.

Proteins are especially important for children and teenagers, whose bodies are not yet fully formed, pregnant women and, of significance to soldiers, those wanting to increase their muscle mass. A diet consistently low in protein would result in the body breaking down tissues, leading to muscle wastage, reduced immunity and weakened vascular and respiratory systems. Foods high in protein are therefore vital for those who wish to build muscle tone and strength.

Fit for Duty

The US military aims to provide its servicemen with nutritionally balanced meals and snacks, no matter where they may be deployed.

Fats and Dehydration

Soldiers have additional considerations in relation to fats. One important factor is that the digestion of fats is very water intensive, using large volumes of body fluids to break the fat down into a digestible form. Normally this fact is not important because adequate fluids are usually available, and professional military units have rehydration schedules in place. But in military survival situations, particularly in arid regions, water can be very hard to come by. Here the soldier must limit, if water supplies are seriously low, his consumption of fatty foods. If you can, eat foods with a high water content, especially fruits or vegetables such as watermelon, tomatoes, cucumber or grapefruit. But if serious dehydration is setting in the soldier should avoid eating anything at all - a human can survive for two or three weeks without food, but only a matter of a few days without water.

Proteins can be found in a variety of foods, such as meat, fish, eggs, dairy products, nuts and seeds. The recommended daily intake of protein is '8 g protein for every 20 lb of body weight' (Harvard School of Public Health), or 10–35 per cent of the daily calorie consumption.

Fats

A certain amount of fat in the diet is essential to good health, although some fats are better for you than others, and some have little or no nutritional value. Fats, or lipids, provide the body with stores of energy and insulate us from the cold. Fats are made up of a group of compounds including fatty acids and glycerol. They can be separated into two main groups:

- **saturated fats**, which come largely from animal fats and can lead to obesity and heart problems;
- **unsaturated fats**, which are more often found in vegetable or fish oils.

Unsaturated fats have more beneficial properties, such as helping to lower cholesterol and keeping your heart healthy (omega-3 fatty acids found in fish oils are especially good for this). However, neither type of fat should be consumed in overly large quantities in a normal diet. The fats naturally found in foods high in carbohydrates and proteins are often enough to provide the energy and insulation we need.

Processed foods and ready meals often contain a high percentage of fats, including trans fats. Trans fats are not commonly found in nature, but occur when fats are processed in food production such as margarine. These fats can raise cholesterol and increase your risk of coronary disease, and should be avoided. The recommended daily intake of fats is 20–35 per cent of the daily calorie consumption. You may want to increase your fat intake if you are intensively training and burning off a large amount of calories. It is also recommended to boost fat stores in the body if you are living or working somewhere very cold, as cold climates expend more body energy than temperate climates (your body burns energy maintaining a constant core temperature).

Vitamins and Minerals

Often defined as micronutrients, foods rich in vitamins and minerals should make up a substantial part of your diet. Both are essential to a healthy body, as they are not synthesized and so must be provided by diet. Vegetables and fruits are the best source of vitamins and minerals, and each has different benefits to different people. The most beneficial ones are explained below. While supplements are readily available, the benefit of processing micronutrients in this form

Vitamin	Optimum dosage (RDA)	Foods rich in vitamin	Benefits
Vitamin A (Retinol)	700–900mcg	cod liver oil, liver, eggs	good vision, skin, teeth and bone health
Vitamin B1 (Thiamine)	1.0–1.2mg	rice bran, yeast, pork	healthy organs, especially nervous system and heart
Vitamin B2 (Riboflavin)	1.0–1.3mg	meat, eggs, bran	healthy metabolism
Vitamin B3 (Niacin)	14–16mg	meat, eggs, grains	healthy metabolism, increased tolerance to cold
Vitamin B5 (Pantothenic acid)	5mg	meat, whole grains, legumes	healthy metabolism
Vitamin B6 (Pyridoxine)	1.2–1.7mg	meat, dairy products	red blood cell production, brain performance
Vitamin B7 (Biotin)	30mcg	meat, dairy products, eggs	healthy cell growth, production of fatty acids
Vitamin B9 (Folate/Folic acid)	400mcg	leafy green vegetables, fortified cereals and bread	healthy DNA and cell growth
Vitamin B12 (Cobalamins)	2.4mcg	liver, eggs, fortified cereals	healthy brain and nervous system
Vitamin C (Ascorbic acid)	75–90mg	citrus, most fresh foods	antioxidant properties
Vitamin D (Calciferol)	600–800IUs	cod liver oil, sunlight	healthy bones
Vitamin E (Tocopherol)	15mg	wheat germ oil, vegetable oil, seeds	healthy nerve and cell production
Vitamin K (Phylloquinone)	90–120mcg	leafy green vegetables	healthy bones, coagulation properties

is unconfirmed. Most professionals agree that the best way to get enough micronutrients is through diet. The body naturally absorbs and stores micronutrients as it breaks down and digests the food that you eat.

Vitamins are needed to ensure healthy skin, bone and muscle production, as well as to prevent against diseases such as anaemia, scurvy, dermatitis, beriberi and rickets (many of these are conditions very rare in developed countries). Currently there are 13 universally recognized vitamins (see tables).

Minerals are needed for healthy red blood cell production (especially important in women), keeping bones and muscles strong, healthy heart and digestive systems and, of course, keeping your brain fit. They also aid the absorption of some minerals.

Minerals are split into seven major minerals and several trace minerals. Those with specific dietary requirements may need other minerals in small quantities.

While a soldier should try to take enough of all the micronutrients, the following vitamins and minerals are especially important for brain health: vitamin E, vitamins B12 and B6, folic acid (vitamin B9) and magnesium.

Important Minerals

Mineral	Optimum dosage (RDA)	Foods rich in mineral	Benefits
Calcium	1000mg	dairy products, eggs, fish, leafy green vegetables	healthy muscles, bones, heart and digestion
Chloride	3–3.8g	table salt	production of hydrochloric acid in the stomach
Magnesium	310–420mg	dark green vegetables, raw nuts, tomatoes	healthy bones, protection against neurotoxins
Phosphorus	700mg	dairy products, red meat, fish	bone and cell production, processing energy
Potassium	4700mg	bananas, tomatoes, legumes	healthy cell function
Sodium	1500–2300mg	table salt, sea vegetables, milk	electrolytes, healthy cell function
Sulfur	trace (no RDA)	high protein foods, meat, fish	amino acid production

Trace minerals			
Mineral	**Optimum dosage (RDA)**	**Foods rich in mineral**	**Benefits**
Copper	900mcg	spinach, greens, seeds, nuts	enzyme production
Iodine	150mcg	sea vegetables, eggs, iodized salt	healthy thyroids, antioxidant
Iron	8–18mg	red meat, leafy green vegetables, oily fish, eggs, beans, grains	healthy cell production
Manganese	1.8–2.3mg	brown rice, beans, spinach, rye	enzyme production
Selenium	55mcg	brazil nuts, meat, fish	antioxidant
Zinc	8-11mg	eggs, red meat, scallops, beans	enzyme production

It is equally important not to take too much of any vitamin or mineral. If you do decide to take supplements, ensure that they do not contain more than 100 per cent of the recommended daily allowance (RDA) per tablet.

Vegetables and fruits are also an important source of dietary fibre, as are some carbohydrates that are also essential for healthy digestion. Fibre is necessary to keep the digestive system healthy. It also releases energy slowly, so that blood sugar levels do not fall or rise too sharply, causing lethargy, and is thought to reduce the risk of cardiovascular disease and colorectal cancer. A diet low in fibre can mean greater risk of infections, heart disease and irregular bowel movements.

The Importance of a Balanced Diet

As discussed, eating most of your food from one category will not give your body everything it needs to perform at optimal physical and mental ability. The US Government recommends the following amounts of food from each category a day, based on the percentages of total daily calories (see opposite).

Aiming to follow these guidelines will help you to consistently perform to your best physical and mental abilities, while enabling you to remain in peak health.

While not every meal needs to contain a balance of each category, you should aim to eat the appropriate amounts of each food group every day for long-term optimum health. The US Government guidelines are followed by the military, with Meals Ready to Eat (MRE), the standard ration packs for deployed military forces, each being made up of approximately 1250 calories, of which at least 13 per cent is protein, 36 per cent fat and 51 per cent carbohydrates. Each MRE also aims to provide one-third of the recommended daily allowance (RDA) of micronutrients. Three MREs are provided a day. Note that the amounts of each category differ slightly to the civilian guidelines,

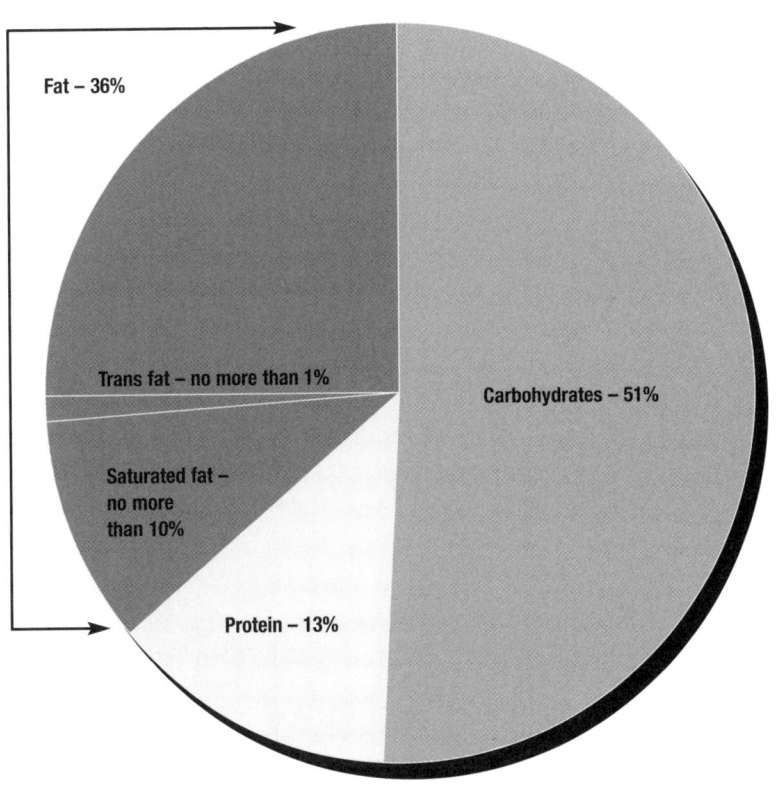

Fat – 36%

Trans fat – no more than 1%

Saturated fat – no more than 10%

Protein – 13%

Carbohydrates – 51%

due to the vastly increased physical activity of those in the military (there is more on MREs below).

Salt and Sugar

While monitoring your general food intake, be aware of hidden or added ingredients such as salt (sodium) and sugar. Both items are found naturally in foods and should only be added as a minimum. The recommended daily allowance of sodium is a maximum of 2300mg a day (roughly one teaspoon of table salt). It is easy to eat too much sodium, as it is often added during production of many processed foods, so monitor amounts on food packaging and try to decrease the amount you add to your diet. Any foods with sodium levels over 20 per cent should be avoided. Consumption of too much sodium can cause feelings of thirst as well as high blood pressure and other imbalances.

The recommended daily allowance of sugar is 36 g (1.3 oz, or nine teaspoons) for men and 20 g (0.7 oz, or five teaspoons) for women. Again, sugars are naturally occurring, so try to avoid adding them to foods as flavouring. Beverages, especially soft drinks, can be very high in sugar. One 355 ml (12 oz) can of carbonated cola drink contains around 39 g (1.4 oz) of sugar – much more than the daily allowance in just one small can. Continually ingesting too much sugar, especially the refined sugars used in

Pocket Foods

Sweets, grains, nuts, dried fruit, etc. are excellent sources of energy. A combination of these snacks provides both simple and complex carbohydrates, which are essential for optimum mental performance during prolonged training.

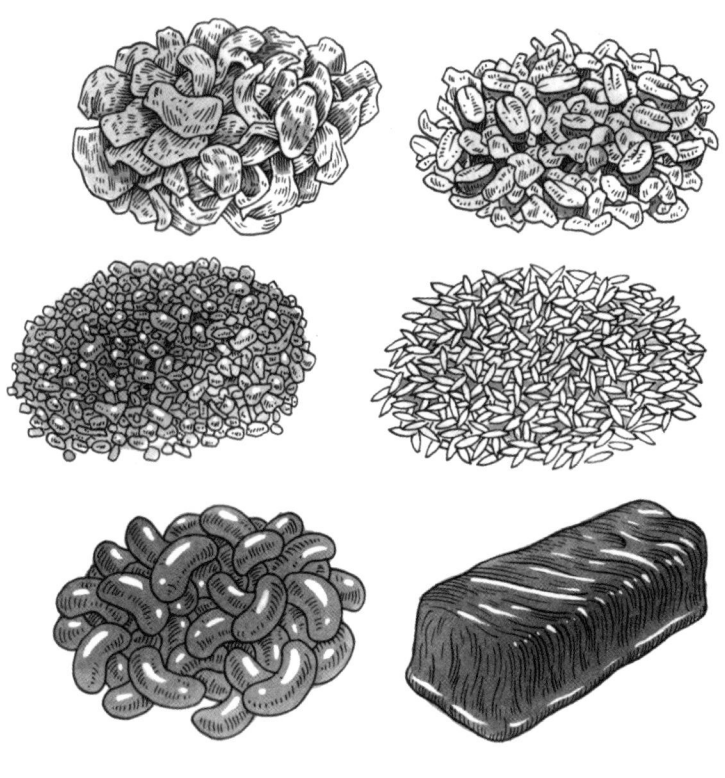

soft drinks and confectionary, can increase the risk of obesity, diabetes, cardiovascular disease and tooth decay.

To soldiers, with their uniquely active lifestyles, both salt and sugar are vital. You lose sugars as they are converted to energy, so these should be continually replaced during exercise. Sodium is lost through sweat, so it also needs to be replaced if you are to continue to perform to your best ability, especially when on operations or exercises that last longer than a day. Anyone engaged in physical activity for over one to three hours should begin to replace lost sodium. Amounts lost through sweat are highly individual, affected by levels of fitness, genetics, weather conditions and physique. You will need to keep an eye on your input to find the right balance for you. As a guideline, aim for an intake of around 400–800mg of sodium per litre (1.75 pints) of water drunk.

Military Diet

Having looked at general dietary recommendations, we now turn in greater detail to specifically military

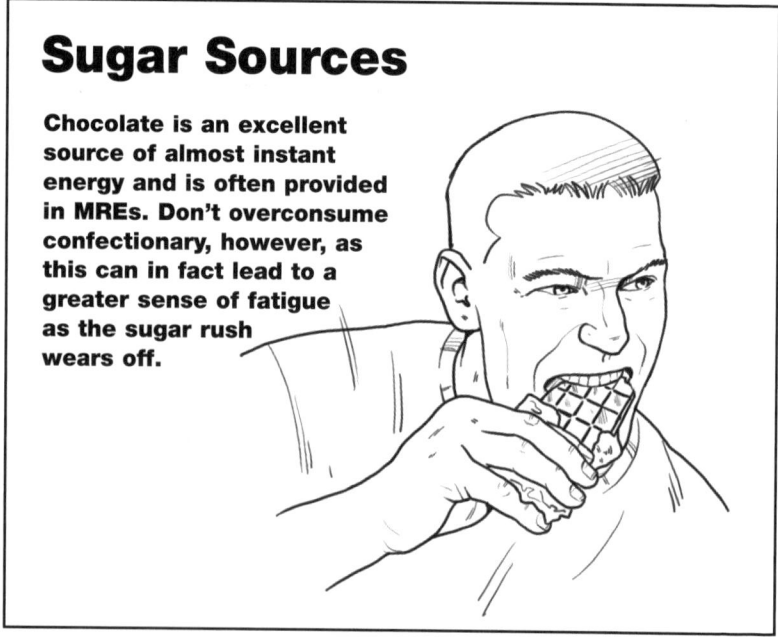

Sugar Sources

Chocolate is an excellent source of almost instant energy and is often provided in MREs. Don't overconsume confectionary, however, as this can in fact lead to a greater sense of fatigue as the sugar rush wears off.

Army Canteen

Eating together can unite servicemen and women, even if only to bond over how unpalatable their rations are. The importance the military places on a good, balanced diet highlights how vital it is for maintaining optimal mental endurance.

diets. For a member of the elite forces, dietary requirements are radically different from the average civilian diet, which is based on a moderately active lifestyle and an average of 150 minutes of exercise a week. Those in basic training could easily do more than three to four times this amount, increasing to 12-plus hours of physical activity a day under really punishing selection programmes (there is more on training schedules in Chapter 4: Training).

If you are building up your exercise programme, you will need to increase your calorie intake to match the extra amount of calories burned or you will start to lose weight. While this could be your primary goal, ensure that you do not drop below a healthy body mass index (BMI); in this case you will also feel low in energy and may find it hard to maintain momentum. As an average guideline, a male military recruit should eat about 1000 calories more a day than a male civilian, with at least 50 per cent of the foods being carbohydrates to ensure that enough energy comes from food to be burned off in exercise. Rough guidelines for how many calories are burned off during certain exercises are in the table opposite. As you will see, your weight makes a difference to how many calories are burned off.

If, therefore, you are a 90kg (200lb) man going on a four-hour route march, carrying all your equipment, you could burn off between 375 calories (walking – 5.6km/h; 3.5mph) and 635 calories (backpacking) for every hour of activity.

Useful Energy Foods
Do not forget that you need to leave a gap between eating and exercise. It is recommended that you wait at least 30 minutes after eating before engaging in physical activity. This

Military Depot

Keeping soldiers fed and watered depends on good logistics. Working in logistics is one of the most mentally demanding aspects of military life, requiring someone who understands the balance between consumption and supply.

Energy Use

One hour of activity	Calories burned based on weight of 73 kg (160 lb)	Calories burned based on weight of 91 kg (200 lb)
Aerobics (high impact)	530	665
Backpacking	510	635
Basketball	585	730
Boxing	630	725
Canoeing (moderate)	280	350
Circuit training	560	740
Cycling (on flat)	440	520
Football	565	710
Hiking	435	545
Marching	450	530
Martial arts	700	815
Rappelling	560	650
Rock climbing	750	860
Rope jumping	860	1075
Rowing	435	545
Running (8km/h; 5mph)	600	750
Skiing (downhill)	315	390
Stair treadmill	650	815
Swimming (laps, moderate)	520	640
Volleyball	290	365
Walking (5.6km/h; 3.5mph)	300	375
Weight training	365	455

Dry Rations

Dry rations are lighter to transport and often have a shelf-life far longer than wet rations. Here we see various powdered and packaged foods, easily transportable in a pack or pouch. Such rations are rarely to be eaten indefinitely – a complete absence fresh foods will ultimately have a detrimental impact on mental performance.

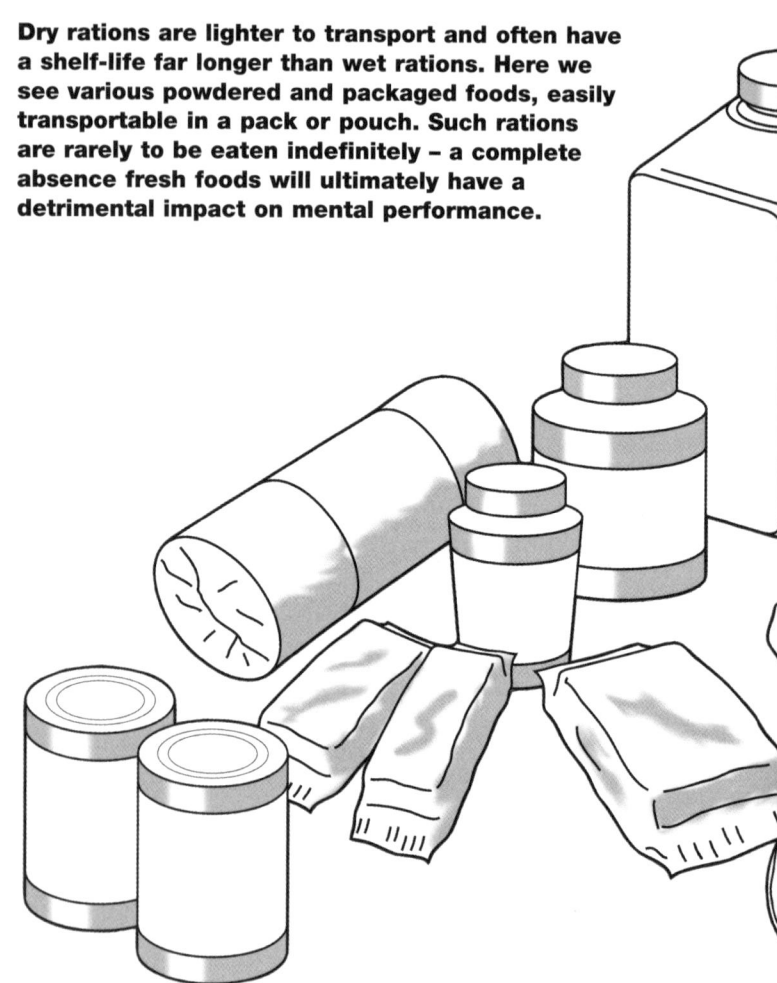

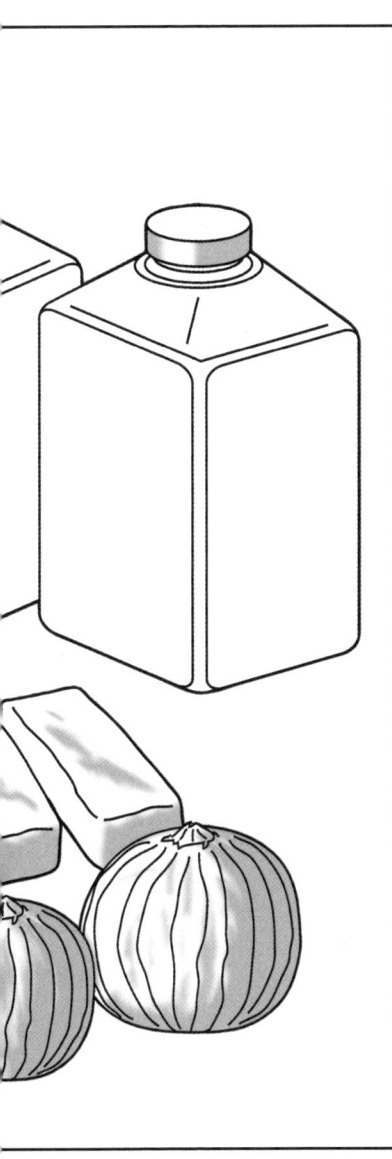

period should be significantly longer if you have had a big meal, which takes on average at least three hours to digest. This also gives your body time to convert the food eaten into energy in the form of glucose. Don't overindulge in the middle of an intensive exercise regime, but instead take small meals or snacks frequently to keep your energy levels topped up.

Some foods (generally simple carbohydrates) have a high glycemic index – they release high levels of energy quickly. These foods can give you a burst of energy and are useful to eat before short bursts of high-impact exercise (up to one hour), but they will not sustain you for long as you will experience a dip in your glucose levels after around 30 minutes to an hour. Foods with high glycemic indexes include bananas, potatoes, honey and glucose.

If you are partaking in endurance sports (over two hours' duration), you should eat foods with a low glycemic index (complex carbohydrates). These provide a more slow and steady release of energy and can keep you going for longer. Low glycemic foods include milk, yoghurt, beans and fructose. If you are likely to be doing endurance exercises for long periods (such as eight-hour route marches with full kit), keep your energy levels up by a combination of both complex and simple carbohydrates.

A popular snack to eat before exercise is a banana. The high level of glucose a banana gives your blood makes it ideal for high-impact exercise of up to an hour. Bananas also contain around 88mg of potassium per 100g (3.5oz) of banana, which is useful to replace the essential salts lost during exercise. Other convenient snacks include yoghurt, trail mix, almonds and energy bars.

If you are exercising first thing in the morning, try to eat at least one of these snacks to boost your energy levels after the overnight fast, if a proper breakfast is not available. When exercising later in the day, aim to make the meal you eat high in carbohydrates, preferably the slow-burning carbohydrates with a lower glycemic index. A banana and a glass of milk is simple, quick and won't be too heavy or uncomfortable to digest. In terms of meals, include wholemeal bread or pasta, fruit and vegetables, brown rice and cereals, but any type of carbohydrates is needed if you are going to be exercising for several hours.

MREs

MREs – Meals Ready to Eat – are the basic field ration packs provided to military personnel when they are on manoeuvres or operations. From a practical and logistical point of view

MREs

CRACKERS

CRACKERS

Meal

Ready-to-eat-individual

The US MRE menus are updated every year, giving servicemen a choice of up to 24 entrees and 150 side dishes and accompaniments, with the aim of making MREs both enjoyable and nutritionally beneficial.

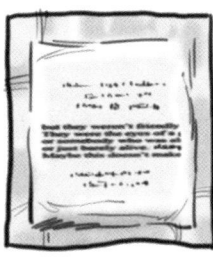

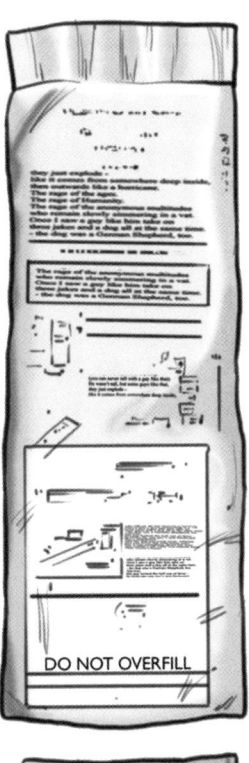

Burning Energy

Walking or jogging with equipment can burn off an average of 500 calories per hour. It is vital that these calories are replaced to ensure that energy levels are continually replenished.

they need to be long-lasting, self-contained and edible under any circumstances. The shelf-life of MREs does depend on the conditions under which they are stored, however, with high temperature having the biggest effect on them. They can last up to five years if stored at 10°C (50°F), but this can drop to just one month if they are stored at 49°C (120°F). The average shelf-life of food stored at around 27°C (80°F) is three years. Boxes also come with a time-temperature indicator to show whether the food inside is still edible.

MREs are officially only sold for consumption by military personnel; however, there are ways to buy

---

MENU 1
Chilli with beans
Corn bread
Cheese spread, jalapeño
Crackers
Ranger Bar
Beverage, carb fortified
Spice, red pepper

Accessory packet A
Spoon
Flameless ration heater
Hot beverage bag

MENU 2
Chicken fajita
Refried beans
Cheese spread, jalapeño
Tortillas
Nuts
Brownie
Irish cream cappuccino
Spice, seasoning blend

Accessory packet B
Spoon
Flameless ration heater

MENU 3
Chicken with noodles
Nut raisin mix w/choc
Peanut butter
Jelly/jam
Wheat snack bread
Beverage, carb fortified
Hot sauce

Accessory packet A
Spoon
Flameless ration heater
Hot beverage bag

MENU 4
Pork sausage w/gravy
Granola
Cheese spread
Crackers
Toaster pastry
Beverage, carb fortified

Accessory packet A
Spoon
Flameless ration heater
Hot beverage bag

Items shown in bold represent changes to the menus, which are updated every year for variety. Special dietary and religious requirements have also been taken into account. There are also variations for hot or cold climates.

them; potentially dubious storage conditions make purchasing them second-hand unwise. There are purpose-made civilian versions such as Sopakco, MREstar and Wornick Eversafe, which aim to provide a similar diet. These are excellent for camping or survival trips, or to experience what living off MREs might be like (soldiers' attitudes to MREs tend to be functional rather than affectionate).

MREs are packaged in cases of 12, with each MRE stored in a tough plastic bag designed to withstand rough handling and exposure to the elements. They also need to be easily transportable when on operations. Each MRE is self-contained, including one main and side dish, with various other sides, condiments, beverages and accessories, including a flameless ration heater (FRH), which heats the main dish up in 10–15 minutes. FRHs work without the use of fire, so are safe to use in the field or even on boats, and they make the MREs much more palatable by warming them.

MREs were first developed by the US military in the late 1970s. Since this time, many changes and improvements have taken place in their contents and pack design. There are currently 24 menus, examples of which are shown on page 39.

The British and Canadian forces use similar rations (24-hour General Purpose ration pack or Individual

Socializing

Even in the field, officers should schedule regular breaks for food and drink, allowing troops to socialize and unwind from the pressures of operations.

Staying Hydrated

Poor hydration has a rapid effect on mental performance, producing confusion, mood changes and apathy. In hot climates in particular, unit leaders should schedule hydration breaks into operations.

Meal Packs respectively) and the average calorie intake for three MREs a day ranges from 3750 to 4200 calories, significantly above the recommended calorie intake for civilians due to the increased activity and calories burned a day. While these meals may not always taste amazing, they are vast improvements on the largely freeze-dried rations supplied to troops prior to their invention. They are also nutritionally balanced and proven to supply soldiers with the right amounts of each food group to sustain them over long periods in the field.

With any major change to diet and exercise, ensure that you give yourself rest days and time off, where you eat for the pleasure of it rather than to fuel your body. There is nothing wrong with this if done occasionally, especially if you have an active lifestyle. Just consider that you may not always need such high amounts of calories on these days.

Fluids

It is hard to overstate the importance of fluid intake for the functioning of the human body and mind. This is as true for mental functions as physical activity. The brain is 70 per cent water, and it uses that water to aid the effective function of all parts of cognition. Studies have shown that just a 2 per cent drop in optimum water levels produce measurable drops in intelligence, logic and emotional state. Therefore, attending to regular rehydration is one of the best ways to ensure peak mental performance.

Looking more broadly, the body must have a certain amount of liquid to keep your major organs healthy and functioning as they should, and to digest any food you eat. If this level of hydration is not maintained, you will quickly begin to feel the effects. Again, it only takes a 2 per cent reduction in bodily fluid for physical symptoms to appear, such as feeling thirsty, decreased or darker urine output, fatigue, headaches, dizziness and a lowering of blood pressure. If fluid loss grows to around 5 or 6 per cent, symptoms can worsen and include nausea, seizure and fainting. Severe dehydration – more than a 15 per cent loss of body fluids – can even be fatal.

Daily Fluid Intake

The minimum suggested amount of fluid intake varies, but it is recommended that at least 2.5 litres (around 4.5 UK pints) of fluids is drunk each day – slightly more than the well-known amount of eight glasses a day. The volumes change dramatically according to exertion and climate. For soldiers deployed on combat operations in desert regions, fluid consumption can be at least double that given for soldiers engaged in light duties in a temperate zone.

This fluid does not have to be just water, but includes anything you may drink that does not contain alcohol. Bear in mind that some caffeinated drinks are diuretic and may make you urinate more, so if you drink five to seven cups of tea of coffee a day, try to increase your levels of water to compensate for any extra fluid loss. While caffeine can be very useful in keeping you focused and alert, it can also make you jittery and anxious if too much is consumed.

If you are very physically active you will sweat more, so you will also need to replace the fluids lost in this way. Aim to increase your fluid intake to at least 3–4 litres (6–8 pints) a day, depending on your level of exertion. This should also be increased if you are in very hot or cold conditions, as you will sweat more due to the heat (as your body tries to cool itself down) and when wearing lots of layers in cold conditions.

Monitor your hydration levels by keeping an eye on the amount you are drinking and how often you need to empty your bladder. If you are going for prolonged periods of over five or six hours without needing to urinate, and if your urine is darker than the normal straw colour (although this differs slightly between individuals), you should aim to replace lost fluids as soon as you can.

Dehydration is easily treated by increasing fluid intake. Water is good, but if you are sweating heavily, you will also need to replace lost electrolytes or sodium. Oral rehydration or sports drinks generally contain sodium and potassium (plus glucose) to quickly replace lost salts and sugars. Low levels of sodium can cause muscles to have trouble functioning properly, which in turn can lead to muscle cramp, so replacing lost salts is especially important during strenuous exercise. There are many of these on the market, including Powerade or Gatorade, some of which are used by the US military in their MREs.

You can make a simple rehydration solution yourself, by dissolving 30ml (6 level tsp) of sugar and 2.5ml (1/2 level tsp) of salt in 1 litre (2 pints) of water. If, for some reason, fluids of any kind are not easily available, ration remaining supplies and avoid heavy exertion in hot weather to minimize the amount lost through sweat.

Alcohol and Drugs

Alcohol has obvious effects on mental performance. As the volume of alcohol consumed increases, there is a corresponding decrease in cognitive functions, powers of judgment, ethical reasoning, communication skills and intelligence. Factor these impairments into a combat situation and it is evident why the world's armies have taken such a stern line on alcohol abuse.

Water Containers

Shown here is a selection of water containers used by the US military, such as water bottles and bags, metal canteens, cups and thermos flasks. The amount of fluid carried needs to be adapted for the environment, but 34 litres (6–8 pints) a day is a good general guide for active soldiers.

The Importance of Rehydrating

Continual replenishment of fluids over the course of the day is the best way to stay hydrated. Monitor the behaviour of others in your unit – deteriorating mental performance might be a simple indicator that he or she is dehydrated.

Even the ruddy-cheeked Royal Navy banned the famous rum ration in 1970, fearing that soldiers would make mistakes with complex machinery or fail breathalyzer tests when driving on public roads. More darkly, high alcohol consumption among soldiers has frequently been associated with troops committing atrocities.

A report in *The New York Times* in 2007 observed that 'Alcohol- and drug-related charges were involved in more than a third of all army criminal prosecutions of soldiers in the two war zones [Iraq and Afghanistan] – 240 of the 665 cases resulting in convictions, according to records obtained by *The New York Times* through a Freedom of Information Act request. Seventy-three of those 240 cases involved some of the most serious crimes committed there, including murder, rape, armed robbery and assault, records show.'

Alcohol stays in the bloodstream for many hours, depending on the volume drunk, so self-controlled soldiers avoid heavy drinking the night before operations. This is especially the case with soldiers, sailors or airmen operating complex machinery; a US Air Force fighter pilot, for example, is unlikely to hold his job for long if he is found to have an alcohol problem.

The dehydrating effect of alcohol is another reason why you should avoid it if in training, if you have

Treating Dehydration

Dehydration can be very serious, even life threatening, if not treated quickly. Replacing lost fluids and slowing further fluid loss is of paramount importance. Monitor anyone suspected of being dehydrated, and also ensure that lost salts are replaced in rehydration formulas.

Writing Home

Letter-writing has an important effect on military morale. It helps bridge the sense of isolation a soldier can feel when on a distant and long deployment. All letters should be monitored during combat operations, however, to ensure that the soldier doesn't unwittingly divulge military secrets.

access to it. While expecting soldiers to cut out all alcohol is unrealistic, you should try to avoid it the day before you will be taking a moderate to high amount of physical exercise. You should also not exceed the daily recommendation of 2–3 units (for women) or 3–4 units (for men), which is thought to lower the risk of heart disease, cancer and liver problems. If you do drink alcohol, try to increase the amount of fluids you drink to reduce the chances of dehydration.

Obviously, the cautions for alcohol are magnified when considering illegal narcotics, such as heroin, cocaine and ecstasy. The use of stimulants is discussed below, but suffice to say that the mind-altering states and health problems caused by illegal narcotics render a soldier dangerous to both himself and his comrades.

Rest

For a soldier, rest and recovery is just as important as diet in ensuring peak mental and physical performance. Not for nothing has sleep deprivation been used as torture. It was used, for example, by the Soviets during the Cold War, the Japanese during World War II and the British Army on IRA suspects during the 1970s. The US Government also used this method on terrorist suspects in Guantanamo Bay, to some controversy. Sleep deprivation is thought to make victims more susceptible, break down their mental reserves and level of resistance – even break their will – making them more likely to give away secrets or submit to following the regime of their captors.

Unfortunately, sleep deprivation is part of everyday life for most soldiers in combat zones. The effects are profound. Limited sleep and rest can cause memory loss, headaches, stress, mood swings, anxiety, a decrease in alertness and attention span – even hallucinations or psychosis. Even getting one late night before an intensive patrol can make a soldier feel sluggish, fatigued and emotionally erratic. There are direct and identifiable links between sleep deprivation and casualty rates. An alert soldier might spot the signs of an emplaced improvised explosive device (IED) or a waiting ambush, but a fatigued soldier could miss all the signs until it is too late.

Ideal Sleep Patterns

On average, most people should aim for at least six to eight hours sleep a night. Military realities, however, render such periods of rest a dream for many soldiers. The Marine Corps Recruit Training Regulation advises eight hours of uninterrupted sleep a night. The regulation does not apply to those on guard duty, mess duty, fire or security watch, or night events, when the amount of sleep a night can drop to six hours, although normal levels should be resumed

as soon as possible. This recognition of the importance of sleep suggests that a lack of it can be detrimental or even dangerous. That aside, it is a reality of military life and should be factored in. During the 'Crucible' event (the final test in Marine recruit training), sleep might drop down to only four hours a night.

An extreme solution is the Uberman sleep cycle, based on polyphasic sleep patterns in which you take several shorter sleeps a day: a 20-minute nap every four hours, with no single, prolonged period of sleep. This method, after an adjustment period of several weeks, can prove very effective and productive for some people. Several military leaders were thought to have had polyphasic sleep patterns, such as Napoleon Bonaparte and Winston Churchill, although both were also thought to catch up on sleep when necessary. Polyphasic sleep is therefore a useful method if you are unable to sleep for longer periods every day, but is not recommended for optimum mental and physical performance, certainly not for prolonged periods of weeks or months.

Sleep deprivation can have a utility for military forces, however. Depriving someone of sleep, especially when his or her normal routine is disrupted and the amount of physical activity carried out is increased, is a good way of seeing people at their most susceptible, and

Sleep Deprivation: Effects

The negative effects of sleep deprivation can be felt on both mind and body. At the very least, you may not be as vigilant as usual, which can result in increased risk of dangers when on manoeuvres and operations.

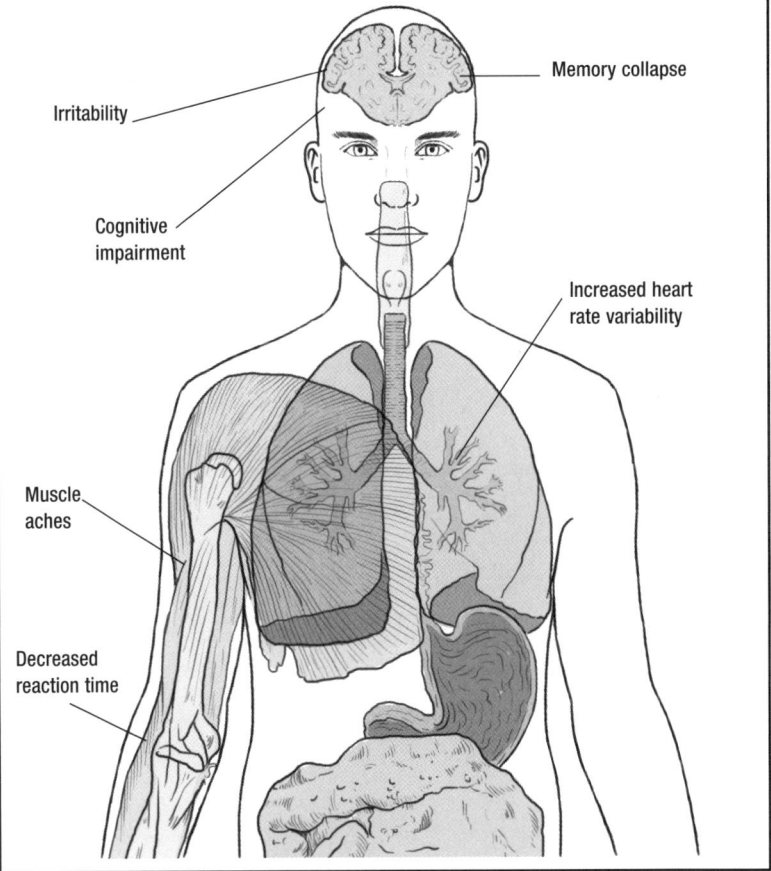

Memory collapse

Irritability

Cognitive impairment

Increased heart rate variability

Muscle aches

Decreased reaction time

Down Time

Soldiers quickly learn to make the most of any brief down time, learning to grab short, refreshing sleeps even in uncomfortable or noisy situations. Studies show that just 20 minutes of rest can compensate for sleep deprivation, as least in the short term.

Restful Sleep

US and UK guidelines suggest a minimum of eight hours of sleep per night. However, US military personnel often need to survive with less sleep. This means that any opportunity for rest and sleep should be taken, and drops in concentration can be countered by stimulants such as sugar and coffee.

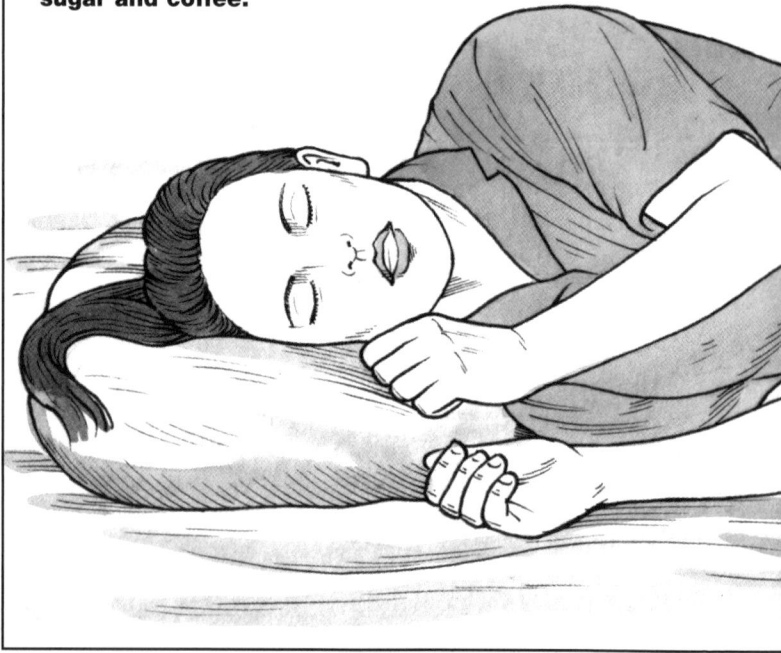

is therefore used in military training to assess personality under stress. It is also a practical way of preparation for the inevitable disruption to sleep, rest and routine that comes with military operations.

While sleep deprivation can be an inevitable part of military life, reports on troops in combat zones suggest that soldiers should get at least seven to eight hours of sleep a night. Even more important here than in

training, any less sleep may result in more accidents and a higher number of ethical misdemeanors, as people become careless and irritable. You may be operating machinery, not to mention being in control of dangerous weaponry, and you will almost certainly have people depending on you to be at your most alert and aware.

The need for sleep is vital, so follow your bodies' instincts and

Field Shower

Field showers have a surprisingly restorative effect on military morale. Continual and long-term poor hygiene can result in a depleted sense of self-worth and motivation.

sleep for as long as you can, when you can. You will need to get used to sleeping in different places. It is easier to fall asleep when you are warm, dry and comfortable, but this might not be the case on many operations.

Sleeping outdoors, inside a vehicle or surrounded by others in close quarters may become the norm. If you have trouble falling asleep, project yourself mentally into a quiet, safe and peaceful place. Imagine it with as much detail as you can, and slowly let yourself drift into it.

Sleep Problems
It may not just be external factors that interrupt your rest. If you have trouble dropping off, or find yourself waking up and not falling back to sleep quickly, you need to think about why this is happening. It could be a physical factor, such as taking caffeine too late in the day (avoid stimulants in the hours before sleep, if you can), or it could be a symptom of underlying worry or stress (perfectly understandable on combat operations).

You might be worried about some aspect of your performance during training and become overtired as you test yourself, or be thinking about what the future will hold. These are valid concerns and need addressing directly. Talk about your issues with an authoritative, calm person, so you can see the problem more objectively (it is hard to think clearly when you are exhausted).

One technique for handling pressures is, just before you go to sleep, to write down everything you are going to do the next day to resolve your problems. The list of action will reassure you, before you go to sleep, that your problems are going to resolve themselves. Training yourself to look at things positively can be tricky and feel false at first, but it is a muscle to be exercised that becomes stronger over time. Chapter 3: Mental Tools deals with how to train and strengthen your brain in this regard.

It is not just sleep that is important. It is vital to make time to do things you enjoy when you can, such as reading, listening to music, playing sports or pursuing hobbies. The mental shift in gear can lower blood pressure, bring focus back to a problem and give you something else to think about. In short, a soldier must never neglect the value of rest and sleep; cutting back on both indefinitely will ultimately make him a worse soldier.

Stimulant Use in War

Since the birth of modern pharmaceuticals, many studies have been conducted on the use of chemical stimulants in wartime, most extensively on German troops during World War II. To deal with the

Stimulants, Drugs and Alcohol

The less you use drugs, chemical stimulants and alcohol, the sharper your mental performance will be over time. It is important not to use these substances as crutches for alleviating stress or worry.

massive fatigue that came with life on the Eastern Front, soldiers were given Benzedrine (amphetamine) and also Methedrine (Pervitin), the latter a type of restorative drug that stimulates the brain and decreases the need for sleep and feelings of tiredness.

The studies (performed in laboratories as well as in the field) showed that the use of such restorative drugs could be useful when dealing with an immediate threat, but not if the emergency situation was likely to last longer than 12 hours, and not given in large numbers to troops.

For the German Army, it is thought that up to 200 million Pervitin pills were distributed between 1939 and 1945, with hundreds of thousands of soldiers using them on a long-term basis. Although there could be short-term survival benefits for some soldiers, for the most part these pills did not improve combat performance due to the effects of mental distortion. Long-term use led to illness and addiction in many.

Modern Practices

Modern military forces have thankfully moved away from such indiscriminate use of stimulants. Yet the demands of combat operations in Iraq and Afghanistan have seen US forces distribute stimulants in significant quantities.

Documents obtained under the Freedom of Information Act by *The New York Times* in 2010 show an increase in expenditure on stimulants from $7.5m in 2001 to $39m in 2010 from . It also shows an increase in the number of Ritalin and Adderall prescriptions issued for active-duty personnel of nearly 1000 per cent in five years. These drugs release norepinephrine, a stimulant that increases alertness and memory function, and both are used in the civilian world to treat attention deficit hyperactive disorder (ADHD) and narcolepsy. There is concern, however, that the drugs' improvements in emotional memory could increase the severity of post-traumatic stress disorder (PTSD) in soldiers confronted by horrific events.

It is never recommended that you take chemical stimulants, unless you are prescribed them by a medical professional, and only under extreme circumstances. If you do take them, observe the mental and physical effects closely and ask your friends to tell you honestly if they notice any worrying mental changes. Discontinue use, in consultation with your physician, if adverse symptoms arise. Meanwhile, rely on all the traditional stimulants where possible – coffee, tea, sugary snacks, good meals and rest. Keeping your body in optimal shape and condition keeps your mind focused, driven and sharp.

US Army Intelligence Report on the use of Benzedrine

(a) The valuable effect of Benzedrine* to individuals engaged in war operations is to reduce the desire for sleep, and the fatigue which results in loss of efficiency and makes difficult the continuation of essential duties.

(b) Circumstances may thus arise in which the administration of Benzedrine may be advantageous for skilled personnel when they are severely fatigued and unable to continue at a reasonable level of efficiency without an additional stimulus.

The use of Benzedrine should be confined to emergencies or crises, and it should not be taken regularly.

The decision to give Benzedrine must only be made in circumstances when there is reasonable expectation that the emergency will be at an end within 12 hours.

(c) No person whose duties involve the making of difficult decisions should be permitted to take Benzedrine in a crisis unless he has tested his reactions to it previously.

(d) Benzedrine must not be given indiscriminately to large bodies of troops.

(e) A single dose should not exceed 10 mg. A dose of 5 mg may be repeated once or even twice at intervals of four to six hours.

(f) The administration of Benzedrine should be under the control of a medical officer.

—US War Department, *Tactical and Technical Trends*, No.11
(5 November 1942)

The challenges of military service begin for most recruits on day one of their basic training. At least in professional armies, training programmes are designed specifically to pressure-test the candidate, to show his real personality under extreme physical and mental conditions.

What is of particular interest to the instructors is to see how the recruit will act at the point of exhaustion. If he simply shuts down and stops thinking, he is unsuited to a military career. If he stays focused, keeps motivated and considers his actions at all times, then he has the makings of a fine soldier. This chapter is about how to stay in this second mental state.

How Your Mind Works

At a basic level, your brain controls the involuntary or unconscious functions of your body to keep you alive. These functions include heart rate, respiration, blood pressure, regulation of body temperature and digestion. Your central nervous system (made up of the brain, spinal cord and nerves) controls movement

....

Military service can involve the most stressful situations anyone can experience, yet by controlling mental processes, a soldier can limit the negative effects of stress, even making it work positively for him.

3

Being a serving soldier is mentally demanding. The challenges can range quickly from prolonged boredom to sheer terror. Effective mental management is essential.

Mental Tools

The Body's Nervous System

The body's nervous system is an extremely complex work of biological engineering, yet even for the non-scientist a basic comprehension of its functions can help in understanding the full spectrum of mental performance. In essence, the human nervous system is broken down into two parts:

• Central nervous system. This consists of the brain and the spinal cord, and is the core of the human body's mental and physical functions.

• Peripheral nervous system. This system is itself divided into two parts: the somatic nervous system, which sends sensory information to the central nervous system and motor nerves connected to skeletal muscle; and the automonic nervous system, which is responsible for controlling the smooth muscle of organs and glands.

As we can see from this brief outline, a large part of the nervous system's functioning is devoted to unconscious processes and the maintenance of basic body functions. It is for this reason alone that diet and mental function are intimately connected – the better the diet, the better the functions of the body are maintained. It also reminds us that mind and body are a holistic system – mental problems often have physical solutions, and vice versa.

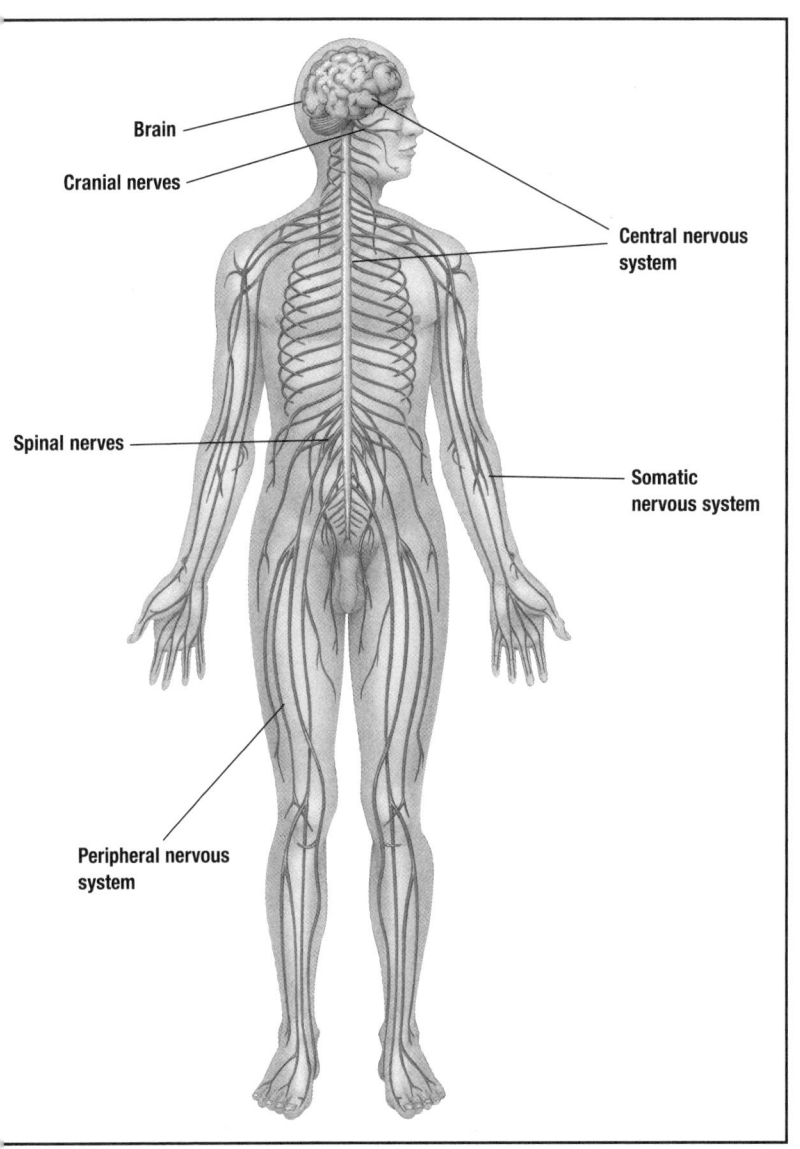

Brain

Cranial nerves

Central nervous
system

Spinal nerves

Somatic
nervous system

Peripheral nervous
system

Brain Spheres

The human brain controls involuntary and voluntary physical processes, as well as being an amazing tool that enables people to perform great feats of bravery and resilience in times of severe stress.

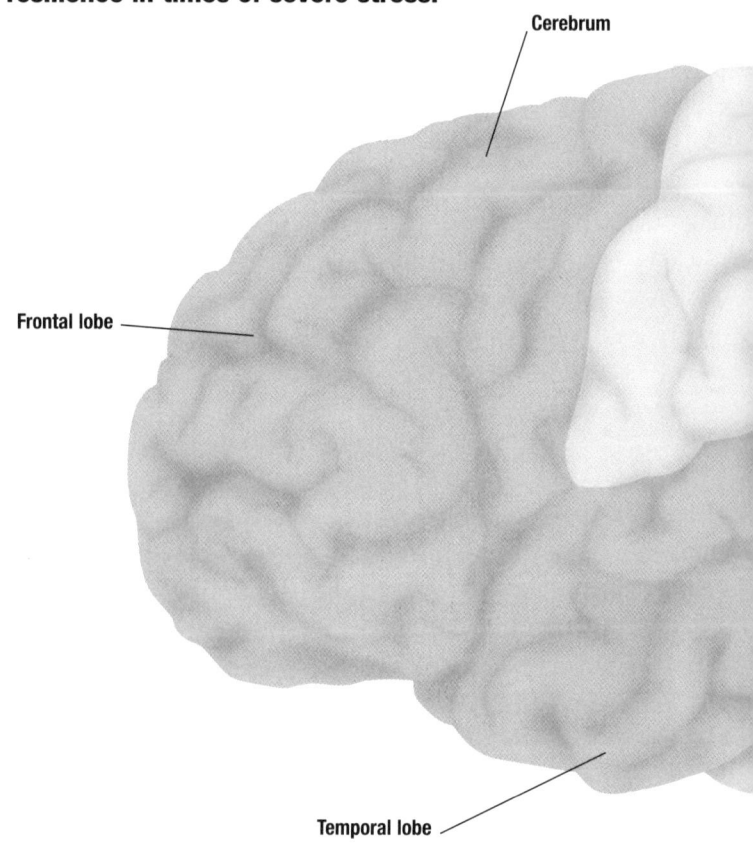

Cerebrum

Frontal lobe

Temporal lobe

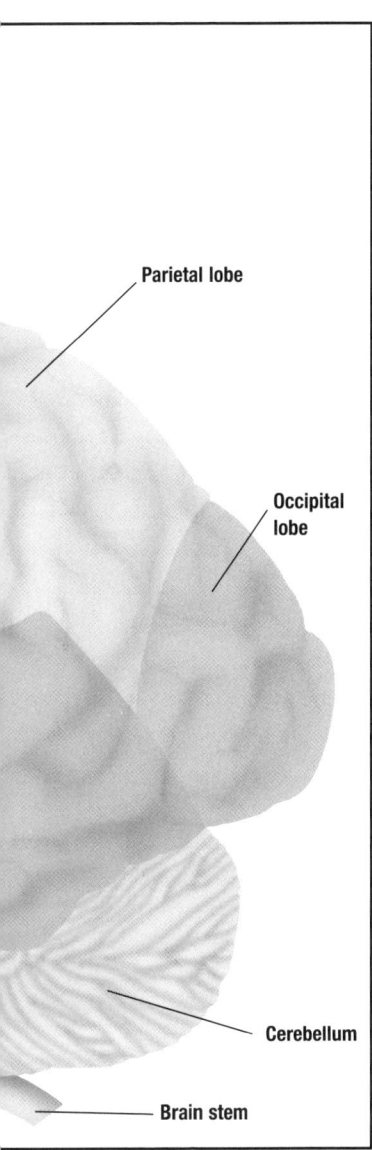

Parietal lobe

Occipital lobe

Cerebellum

Brain stem

and sensory processing, such as vision, hearing and taste. The cerebrum, which is much larger in humans than other animals, controls thought processes and emotions, and stores memory. Simply put, it is that cerebrum that makes humans different to animals, which mainly perform instinctive actions necessary for survival and basic socializing.

The cerebrum is split into several areas, including the parietal lobe (responsible for language acquisition and processing as well as sensory functions), the frontal lobe (for short-term memory, motor skills and higher cognitive functions), the occipital lobe (for processing visual information) and the temporal lobe (for processing auditory information and long-term memory). Parts of the cerebrum are also responsible for fine motor skills and movements, visceral muscle control, taste information, social and sexual behaviour, emotional behaviour and personality.

Understanding how your brain works will help you use it to its fullest potential. One basic point, outlined further in Chapter 4: Training, is that your natural reactions to events can be programmed by repetitious and realistic training. This is why Special Forces soldiers train hour upon hour, day after day, with their small arms, responding rapidly with bursts of aimed fire as targets are presented. They repeat this process so many times that it becomes

Judging Distance

This image shows how a soldier forms a 'telescope' with his fist to judge the distance between himself and the aircraft he is monitoring. Using this simple technique filters out background disturbance that might otherwise distract the viewer. The greater the space around the plane, the further away it is.

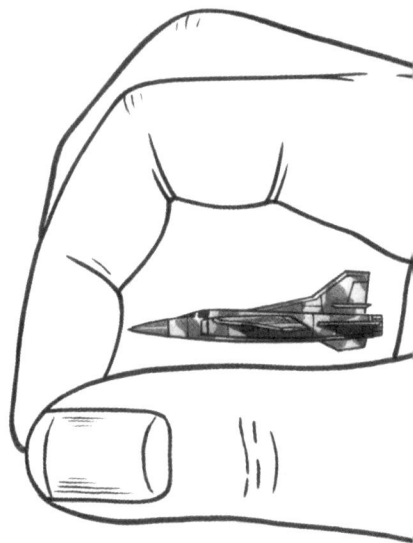

instinctive, an action they apply in combat even when the stress of the situation is affecting their conscious mental processes.

Another point this chapter will reinforce is that psychological studies have shown that the way you hold your body and carry yourself physically actually leads your mental state, not the other way around. In short, if you act confident and

proficient, you will most likely become confident and efficient. These principles will recur in this chapter, but also underpin many other chapters in this book.

Mental Focus
Although armies vary in terms of their entry requirements, all professional armies look for certain core attributes. The US Army, for

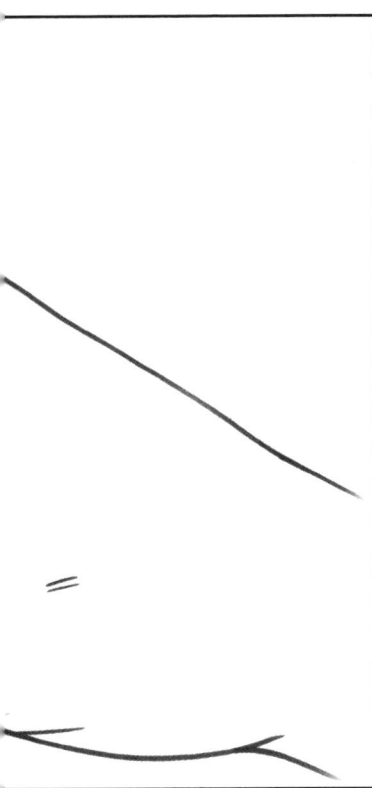

Readiness Members of the Armed Forces must be ready and able to report for military assignments on short notice (see www.bls.gov/ooh/Military/Military-Careers.htm).

These simple formulas conceal a broad range of mental and physical demands. For example, the description of the mental preparedness sounds simple enough, but the oblique reference to 'stressful situations that can occur during military operations' can include watching friends injured or killed in front of you, as well as facing up to your own imminent death. It is estimated that 12–20 per cent of Iraqi soldiers suffer from PTSD due to their experiences on active duty, indicative of the harrowing effect of modern warfare (more on this in Chapter 7: Trauma and Shock). Similarly, being 'able to report for military assignments on short notice' can mean being pulled away from family and friends in just a few hours and sent on a combat deployment that could last many months.

Being able to face these issues and adapt to them is essential to mental survival as a soldier. Maintaining a state of 'mental readiness' is something that elite forces learn in training, with the objective of confronting normal, everyday activities and stressful combat situations in the same alert and focused state of mind.

example, expects recruits to have the following qualities:
Mental preparedness Armed Forces members must be mentally stable and able to withstand stressful situations that can occur during military operations.
Physical fitness Military members must be physically fit to participate in or support combat missions that may be difficult or dangerous.

Combat Readiness

These soldiers observe an enemy stronghold, knowing that they could be attacked at any second. Note how each soldier is assigned a specific sphere of observation, meaning they do not have to handle too much at any time.

Breaking Down Barriers

The military wants its soldiers to demonstrate the ability to succeed, whether in peacetime duties or in a combat scenario. Barriers to success can be split into two main categories: external and internal. External barriers are those that interfere directly in the time available to perform an important task. They could be anything from a busy week at work, feeling under the weather or family responsibilities, meaning you do not have the time or inclination to continue physical training or meet your self-set training or preparation goals. Sometimes you just have to acknowledge that you cannot control every factor, so try not to get stressed or angry about things that are truly beyond your control, such as bad weather, accidents or sickness.

When events are within your control, follow effective principles of time management, as follows:
1) Rank all the tasks you have to do in order of importance.
2) Focus the bulk of your efforts – at least 80 per cent – on the most important tasks. (If you can, delegate the least important tasks to a third party.) Allocate specific and definable periods of the day in which you will work on those tasks. Most importantly, define exactly what you want to achieve within the time period.
3) Focus all your efforts on completing tasks, not simply working on them. Create a checklist of tasks and only tick the 'completed' box when you have nothing more to do on that task.

More about effective time management time is discussed in the 'Leadership' section below. Equally important is accepting the fact that sometimes goals remain out of reach for reasons beyond your control. Coalition troops in Afghanistan, for example, have had to get used to fighting hard for a piece of terrain, often suffering casualties in the process, but then are forced to relinquish the ground the very next day because of manpower limitations. If a soldier dwells obsessively on this fact, he is likely to become extremely demoralized. The lesson is that, as a soldier, you have to focus on immediate priorities and objectives and leave the big picture in the hands of greater political and social forces.

If you get disheartened when events don't go your way, you will find great difficulty in remaining positive during your service. Adaptability is very important in military life, where you can never predict entirely how things turn out even with the most thorough planning. Such is what military theorist Carl Philipp Gottfried von Clausewitz (1780–1831) termed the 'fog of war'.

Time Management

Checklists can save you time and energy, as well as allowing you to focus your thoughts and prioritize important tasks.

Frustration, stress and other negative mental states form your internal barriers. If you are finding that you are continually downsizing your goals, making excuses or putting things off, you need to stop, review what you have achieved and revisit where you want to be. Every step you have already made should be viewed as a triumph, no matter how small. Aim to look upon barriers as future triumphs, rather than overwhelming crises too huge to be overcome.

Revisit your goals and remind yourself what you wanted to achieve in the first place. Then, take stock of where you are and what you need to do, including any barriers that may now be standing in your way, and plan how you can move forward from your current position to where you want to be. This might be successfully completing elite forces training, gaining experience of combat or getting a promotion. Often, the process of setting out your plan and rearranging it to better suit your lifestyle will make you feel calmer and more in control.

Acting and Reacting

Consistent behaviour, especially in times of combat, is very important. However, the instinctive part of your brain can take over in times of severe

---

Word Challenge

An example of a language puzzle used by Special Forces recruitment papers. Try to crack the code of this puzzle to reveal a comprehensible sentence.

Vjg iriqc jt up vjg ohiw jpero

(See answer on page 308)

stress or anxiety, meaning that your actions may be irrational or even dangerous. Your first instinct may be to escape from threat and save yourself, but this might be at the cost of leaving your comrades in danger. (An Iraq War veteran interviewed by the author said that in his first experience of combat, almost every soldier's reaction is to curl up behind cover and 'wet his pants'.)

The critical point in combat is to 'keep those actions clear', as Tom Hanks memorably said to the soldiers under his command during the blistering opening combat scene of *Saving Private Ryan*. A few seconds of considered thinking could make the difference between victory and disaster. Consider the following scenario. You are a senior NCO in a vehicle convoy in Afghanistan. The convoy comes under ambush and several of your men are killed or wounded. You have to get your convoy out of the 'kill box', but one vehicle, full of soldiers, has been disabled behind you. Do you keep everyone moving, and risk leaving the single vehicle and its occupants behind, or return through the fire to pick them up?

Although the situation doesn't allow the luxury of prolonged thinking, a few seconds of dispassionate consideration will make a critical difference. Above all, you have to make an actionable decision to focus the actions of you

and your men. Information you might weigh up includes:

- the weight and direction of incoming fire.
- your ability to deliver return fire.
- whether you have access to close air support (CAS).
- whether another vehicle is in close proximity to the disabled vehicle to make a rescue attempt.
- whether turning back to pick up the men might jeopardize the overall mission.

By taking a few seconds to assess the situation, then acting rationally instead of reacting with your gut feeling to the heat of the situation, you are more likely to make an informed choice. This is, of course, easier said than done, but good training will go a long way to inculcating the correct range of responses. If you let yourself react without thinking, you may not have considered the most appropriate course of action for everyone. Furthermore, if you were wounded or killed, your men might be left without a leader, making them much more likely to be killed or wounded in turn. Most servicemen and women would rather be dependent on the soldier who makes quick but rational decisions, instead of someone who simply reacts to stressful situations without thinking.

In the above scenario, your response might pan out as follows:

Measured Response

Here a US patrol slowly surrounds its vehicle to survey every angle visible to them. Weapon sights can be a useful tool for controlling observation, by using them to explore each aspect of the terrain systematically.

1. Direct the vehicles at the front of the convoy to keep moving out of the 'kill box'.

2. Instruct two units of troops to suppress the enemy with heavy return fire, while you take a single vehicle back to effect a rescue mission.

3. Instruct any CAS assets to strike the enemy positions.

4. Once the stranded soldiers are retrieved, move at speed out of the kill zone while maintaining return fire from vehicle-mounted weapons.

The important part about any plan you form is that it must be simple – too many interdependent stages just invites disaster – and it must be easily transferred to other soldiers in simple language. 'Keep those actions clear' does appear to be a solid mantra.

Effects of Stress

Stress is the biggest inhibitor of clear thinking. It is an involuntary response to a perceived threat, which causes your nervous system to release hormones that prepare your body to respond to danger. This happens very quickly and elicits increased heart rate and blood pressure, muscle contractions and quickening of the breath. The problem is that the stress reaction channels more blood to muscles, heart and lungs, and consequently drains it from the brain – the very organ you need to sustain clear thought.

Panic Response

Humans are programmed to react instinctively to threat. This instinct to fight or flee from a dangerous situation is made worse by prolonged exposure to stress. Military training aims to reduce this instinct to panic.

Effects of Stress

Stress can be a soldier's worse enemy. Typical effects include an inability to concentrate, rapid mood swings, depression and insomnia, and need to be dealt with rapidly by team leaders.

Physical effects of stress	Mental effects of stress
Increased heart rate or chest pain	Focusing on the negative
Dizziness and sweating	Irrational behaviour
Nausea or indigestion	Increased temper or irritability
Diarrhoea or constipation	Memory and concentration problems
Nervous habits, such as pacing or talking much more than usual	Impaired judgment
Being prone to illness or pain	Inability to relax or switch off
Eating too much or not enough	Neglecting or refusing responsibilities
Sleeping too much or not enough	Feelings of depression and isolation

Small amounts of stress can be good, as they help us react under pressure and provide motivation and stimulus. In emergency situations, it is this release of hormones (adrenalin and cortisol) that provides the extra burst of strength or speed needed. This response cannot be sustained, however, as neither the body nor mind can keep working at optimal level for sustained periods.

Stress can cause a sensory overload, where judgment and ability to process situations quickly are both impaired. It is therefore vital to have effective stress management, both on an immediate and a prolonged basis.

Dealing with Stress

Despite the body's instinctive response to stress, there are ways to deal with it effectively so that it doesn't become a hindrance to your performance. Awareness of the physical symptoms is your first tool. Even in situations where you need to act quickly, if you notice your stress reaching unmanageable levels, take a few slow, deep breaths from your diaphragm, ensuring that you breathe in and out for roughly equal lengths of time. If you feel your muscles contracting, consciously relax them.

In a non-combat situation, you can take time out by focusing on one or more of your senses, such as visualizing the face of a friend or loved one, the sound of your favorite piece of music or a comforting, familiar smell. If your environment means that your senses are being assaulted with unpleasant sights and sounds, try calling to mind a word or phrase with special meaning for you (there is more on this in the 'Meditation' section later in this chapter), or close your eyes for a few seconds and centre your footing. Anything that, however briefly, removes you from the situation and stress can bring clarity and calm to your thinking and actions.

Another way to handle stress is literally to act relaxed, like an actor playing a role. Imagine yourself being cool, calm and centred, with a confident and assured body posture, then force your body to adopt this position. It might feel artificial at first, but slowly your mind will catch up a little. If you struggle to understand this principle, think of what you do with your body when you are depressed:

- unfocused eyes
- curled-up body positions, such as folded arms and legs or the fetal position
- chin dropped low to the chest
- shallow breathing

It is actually quite hard to be depressed if you adopt the physical opposites of these traits – focused, outward-looking gaze; open, straight body posture; chin raised; breathing deeply and calmly. Training yourself in this de-stressing technique means that you can limit the negative effects of stress almost straight away. The instinctive responses learned in combat training also prepare soldiers for dealing with stress instantly, and this training is thought to lessen the number who suffer from combat stress reaction (CSR).

Stress Crutches
The US Substance Abuse and Mental Health Services Administration (SAMHSA) has a useful guide for preventing stress in emergency response and public safety workers. Their guidelines can be equally relevant to those in military service, who may be involved in many traumatic events. Knowing what the normal reactions to these events are is the first step to managing your feelings.

Never forget you are not alone in your feelings. Even if it seems as if everyone else is coping better than you, people have different ways of hiding the stress, grief or fear they are feeling. Talk to someone you trust or to an impartial professional about what you have experienced and avoid unnecessarily stressful situations. Keep to your routine wherever possible and carry on doing the things that you enjoy, even if you don't have much energy for things.

Drown Proofing – Coping with Stress

Drown proofing is a highly disorientating experience. This US Navy SEALs training exercise allows instructors to spot those able to manage stress and the instinct to panic.

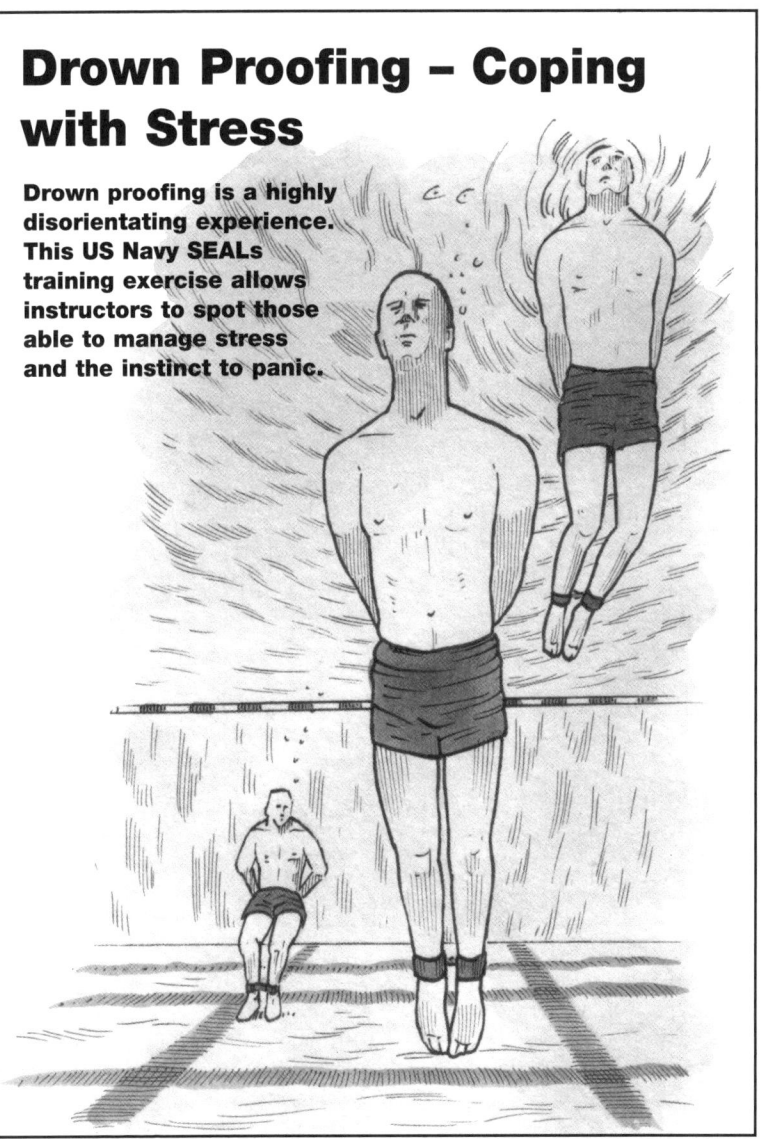

Pressure Testing

A complicated stress-testing technique used by US military research groups was to get soldiers to fill in life assurance forms while aboard a plane apparently about to crash land.

These techniques are especially important if you find yourself becoming dependent on drugs or alcohol as a means of reducing your stress levels or blocking out disagreeable events. While you may feel better in the short term, increases in the amount of alcohol you are drinking or drug-taking (or dependence on either substance) can make life much more stressful in the long term, and can cause

Normal Reactions to a Traumatic Event

No one who responds to a mass casualty event is untouched by it. Profound sadness, grief and anger are normal reactions to an abnormal event.

- You may not want to leave the scene until the work is finished.
- You likely will try to override stress and fatigue with dedication and commitment.
- You may deny the need for rest and recovery time.

damage to health as well as impairment to both physical and mental performance. If you find yourself becoming dependent on prescription drugs or panicking when they run low, taking any form of non-prescription drugs or drinking every day, you need to figure out why this is and how to stop this dependence.

Mental Training Techniques

Training your mind to prepare for and deal with stress effectively before it occurs can minimize its negative effects. It might be tempting for soldiers to think that activities such as visualization and meditation are not for them, but you should look on the following techniques as exercise – just as physical training makes your body stronger, mental training makes your brain stronger. The US military, for example, have incorporated similar techniques for soldiers in Iraq in 2010 as tactics for coping with stress.

Using meditation exercises such as 'mindfulness' can prepare soldiers for the stress of deployment as well as dealing with PTSD and depression after being in combat by being able to better control their moods and feelings. You are likely to experience relatively severe stress at some point in your military career; it is how you react to, deal with and move on from this stress that often defines you as a soldier. Starting to recognize that we can neither change our past nor foresee our future allows us to focus on the present situation and deal with it more positively.

Mindfulness

This US Government news article explains the role of mindfulness:

> Mindfulness is a simple but ancient approach to living, which Western medicine has begun to recognize as a powerful tool for dealing with stress, illness and other medical or psychological conditions, and it can help soldiers in any circumstance, said Army Maj. Victor Won, deputy assistant chief of staff for intelligence in 1st Armored Division's general staff. 'It would be more effective for soldiers to learn and train mindfulness prior to deployment,' Won said, 'since the practice will offer soldiers [a means] to cope with their mental stress before getting into a high-stress environment. However, practicing the meditation on a regular basis will help anyone, no matter where they are.' [...]

The US Army is moving toward developing stress coping methods, Won noted. Mental fitness is similar to physical fitness, he explained. Just as running or lifting weights can improve

Mindfulness in Combat

During combat patrols, soldiers need to train their observational technique, scanning the terrain systematically with their eyes and looking for anything out of the ordinary.

Meditation

For centuries, people have used meditation to bring calm and control over their mental state. It can be particularly effective for clearing the mind after stressful combat situations.

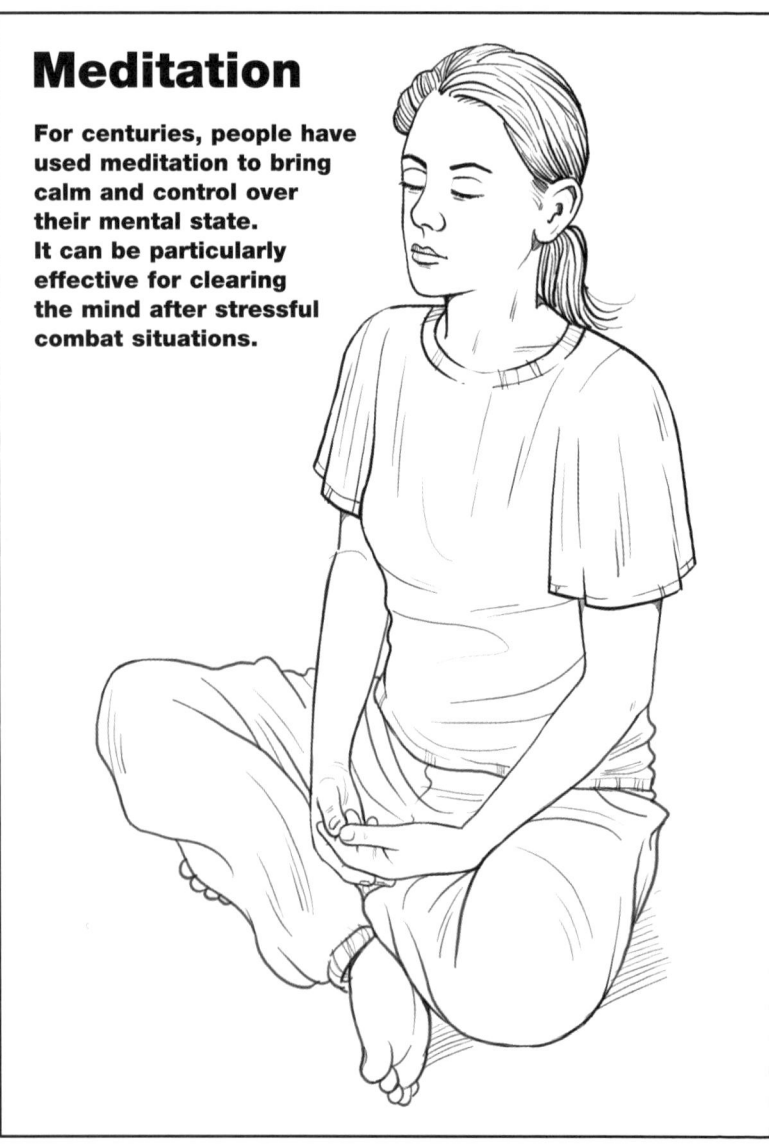

physical fitness, a daily routine of mindfulness will help to strengthen coping mechanisms, making it easier to recognize and react to negative emotions so they don't grow stronger.

> *'Rather than dwelling in the past or the future,' Won said, 'mindfulness is learning to work in the present moment in a less reactive, less judgmental manner.'* (See www.defense.gov/news/ newsarticle.aspx?id=60294_)

The objective of mindfulness is what the military calls 'resiliency', the ability to be mentally strong in the face of repeated hardship and trauma. The specifics of mindfulness training (MT) vary across the army, but common techniques are as follows:

- deep breathing as a simple exercise to reduce stress levels
- the use of calming pieces of music, particularly classical tunes
- visualizing places of safety, giving the soldier somewhere peaceful to go
- focusing on identifying one or two manageable goals in stressful situations, to give clarity amid chaos
- traditional forms of mental training, such as meditation and yoga

These techniques might seem rather 'new age', but reputable scientific studies in elite units such as the US Navy SEALs have shown that mindfulness training increases both 'resiliency' and combat performance.

Meditation Techniques

Meditation is essentially the process of calming or emptying the mind. It is especially useful when there is a lot going on, both around you and inside your head, as it can focus your thoughts and bring clarity:

- Find a quiet place with no distractions where you can sit in comfort, preferably alone.
- Concentrate on breathing deeply and steadily, trying to regulate the length of each breath.
- Relax your muscles one by one, concentrating on each one as you do so. Your aim is to feel relaxed, yet focused, not to go to sleep.
- Concentrate on a word or phrase and let go of other thoughts or worries. This word or phrase could be something like 'Truth', 'Success', or 'I will meet and exceed my targets'.
- Another option is to focus on a picture or image that you have created, such as seeing yourself in a place of peace or achieving a goal.
- Still your mind and keep focusing on your word or image for at least five to 10 minutes, continuing to take deep, even breaths. When other thoughts inevitably crowd in, observe them without emotion, let them go and return to your point of focus.

Self-hypnosis

Self-hypnosis involves settling into a relaxed, alert state by concentrating on breathing and softening the muscles. The soldier then takes himself calmly through whatever situation he is concerned about, a process that also helps him to cope with similar situations encountered in everyday life.

The process of making your mind still takes practice, but as you continue to meditate, you will find that fewer thoughts pop into your head to distract your stillness. This technique, when practised regularly, will result in calmer, more methodical decision-making processes. Build up to longer meditative sessions over time and try different methods. Listening to or playing music, creating artwork, enjoying nature or yoga – especially while focusing on calming your breathing and relaxing your muscles – all allow the mind to focus on something else and reduce stress.

There are many benefits to meditation, not the least that it offers you some brief respite from whatever you may be worried about. This can allow you to see things more clearly, or at least figure out different ways of dealing with a problem that you might have been too stressed to identify before.

Meditation also gives you a break from the self-doubt, guilt and other negative feelings you may experience

as a result of your worries, which people can easily dwell on in tough times. Gaining control over your thoughts and emotions can bring a sense of clarity, allowing you to increase your level of control over other aspects of your life. This clarity and self-control is an important tool for elite soldiers, when other members of the team depend on their ability to perform.

By controlling your mind, you are also exercising control over your body. When you are stressed, the involuntary fight or flight reaction causes your muscles to tense as you prepare to react. The more you remain stressed, the more your muscles contract. You will find it easier to relax your mind if your muscles are also relaxed. Consciously thinking about your muscle state often helps you notice if they are contracted or relaxed; it might also relieve headaches, back pain or stomach complaints, which can be common side effects of prolonged stress.

Positive Thinking

The power of positive thinking should not be underestimated. Having a positive frame of mind and making the best of things can make you a happier, more energized and productive person. It also has important social effects. If you are spending most of your time in close quarters with other people under stressful circumstances, think about who you would rather have with you – someone who always thought negatively and gave up easily, or someone who was upbeat and tried their best to fix problems if and when they occurred? Also think about the person you would rather be.

As with physical preparation and training, the more you practice positive thinking, the easier the habit will become. If you believe that something is impossible to achieve, the chances are that you will unconsciously place obstacles in your way, as you may not have the mental strength to search for alternative ways to overcome the barrier. Mahatma Gandhi (1869–1948) put it this way:

Man often becomes what he believes himself to be. If I keep on saying to myself that I cannot do a certain thing, it is possible that I may end by really becoming incapable of doing it. On the contrary, if I have the belief that I can do it, I shall surely acquire the capacity to do it even if I may not have it at the beginning.

Gandhi warns against self-fulfilling prophecy – a belief in something (even though this belief might not be true) that causes it to be realized. If you believe you are going to ace your military training and excel in the elite forces, you are likely to expend more time and energy in preparing your mind and body than on worrying about it, so you have a greater chance of your belief becoming reality.

There is evidence too that thinking positively can also reduce the physical underperformance and lethargy related to stress or anxiety. Roger Bannister (1929–), the first man to run a mile in under four minutes, is a good example of the power of positive thinking. Prior to him beating the four-minute barrier in 1954, the feat had been thought almost impossible. After Bannister had shown that it was possible, several other runners, now seeing it could be done, also beat the four-minute mile. Bannister showed great dedication and commitment to his sport, continuing to push himself whenever he felt he did not perform to his own high standards, such as in the 1952 Olympics. His years of endurance and positive thinking paid off many times.

In a military context, there are many examples of leaders and soldiers who have achieved

Being in Control

**Operating complex combat technologies requires
advanced training as well as mental composure.
In times of stress, vocalizing your next move can
help you maintain concentration, such as saying out
loud: 'I now need to check the radar for hostile aircraft.'**

Mutual Support

In combat, individual soldiers often rely upon the collective courage of the team to keep them functioning. They must be careful, however, that their need for comradeship doesn't cloud judgement – sticking too close together, for example, presents a greater target for enemy fire.

Positive Thinking Techniques

- When you catch yourself thinking negatively, reverse your thinking so you imagine the positive side of things instead.
- Don't take failure personally; be objective about things and try to learn from mistakes.
- Do not look at things as failures, but as challenges that you are capable of meeting.
- Take control of the situation; if you see yourself as a victim, it is easy to become one, especially as others will treat you this way.
- Smile – literally. Smiling, even when you are not feeling positive, makes us feel better as we associate smiling with feeling good.
- Think back to a time when you felt proud of your actions and achievements and list them. They will remind you of how far you have come already.

seemingly impossible feats through a combination of positive thinking, rigorous training and a defiant attitude. Examples include the English forces at Agincourt in 1415; German parachute forces at Eben-Emael in May 1940; and US Marines and soldiers in Fallujah in 2004. Of course, positive thinking should never be confused with wishful thinking. Being positive still demands absolute realism in planning, intelligence gathering and considering potential outcomes. What it does mean, however, is that once a line of action is chosen, you commit to it in the focused belief that it can and will work.

Just as with the meditation techniques, the more you try positive thinking, the better it can work for you and the more natural it will seem. Consider amalgamating the two techniques, and making your phrase a positive reinforcement of your determination and courage.

Visualization and Imagery

Positive visualization or mental imagery can be a very powerful tool to overcome barriers to success. Visualization works on the basis of the fact that the brain, when faced with a new or stressful situation, looks for the nearest behavioural 'file' in the bank of memories to

Visualization Techniques

Here, a soldier uses visualization to encourage positive thinking. Intense mental focus on achieving your goals makes it more likely that you will overcome challenges in the outside world.

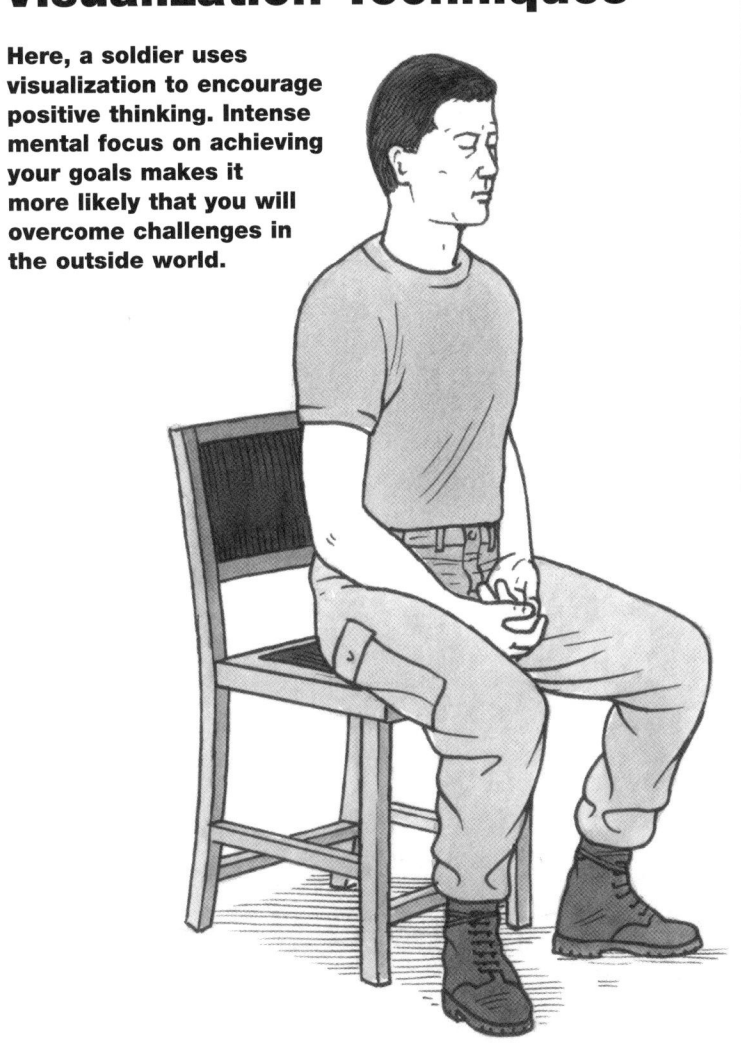

Visualization technique – Coping with Basic Training

In this scenario, you want to use visualization to help you get through the selection process. These same techniques could be used in a variety of situations.

• Spend five minutes relaxing your body to make your mind more receptive and focused.

- Now picture yourself performing through the basic training exercises (obstacle courses, logic test etc) perfectly, focusing on how you feel after every success. Be very clear at the outset about what you want to achieve.

- Start off with five to 10 minutes of positive imagery each day, gradually building up the length of time and varying the images.

- Add detail to your visualizations, such as picturing yourself in your usual training ground and workout kit, the weather and people around you, to make it as real as possible.

- Be realistic – you will feel hot, tired, thirsty, hungry and uncomfortable, so imagine yourself feeling this way, yet still managing to overcome challenges and reach your goals.

direct the response. Visualization works by creating such a file through strong, repeated mental images. Top athletes, such as golfer Jack Nicklaus (1940–) and tennis player Roger Federer (1981–), have used visualization to refine and enhance their game to the highest levels, but it can be useful in many situations, from beating stress to performing consistently well under the pressure of military life.

Visualization begins when you identify something you want to change. Relax your body using the meditation techniques described above, then picture yourself in the problematic situation but performing calmly, successively and confidently. See yourself achieving the goals you desire, and imagine how you feel in doing so. The key to the whole process is to visualize the scene with as much detail as possible, including sights, sounds, colours, smells and sensations of touch. If imagined strongly enough, the brain will not be able to tell the difference between the imagined 'file' and a real one. Furthermore, the imagined picture will provide a model for your physical actions.

Visualization can also help you to overcome fears. If you suffer from a fear of heights, for example, but know that you will have to go up in a helicopter or climb high mountains during your military training, imagine yourself sat in the open door of a flying helicopter, feeling stable, composed and enthralled at the view beneath you. The Special Forces use a similar technique during training to prepare men for live combat situations. As with positive thinking, you can build visualization into your meditation so that you are calming your mind while reinforcing a positive image of yourself.

Confidence and Assertiveness

The more you develop and use these mental tools, the more emotionally resilient you will become. This will increase your confidence, a vital tool in both military and civilian life. You do not need to be overly confident, which can come across as arrogance, but most military leaders appear naturally assured, and so inspire trust in their men. Think about your own experiences with teachers, employers or trainers. It is likely that you were drawn to strong, engaging people who exuded authority and treated you with respect. It is also likely that you were willing to follow these people more readily than those who shouted at you, became angry whenever you made a mistake or seemed unsure of what they were doing.

If you are not a naturally confident person, it can be hard to maintain a bold persona, especially when you are in unfamiliar situations, new to the military or less experienced than

many of the servicemen around you. Imagine the situation of having to clear civilians out of a village that has become a terrorist stronghold. They do not know you or have any reason to trust you. Are they more likely to follow someone who seems to know what they are doing or someone who appears hesitant and unsure? Think about how confident people you know and admire look and act. They act with certainty, determination and commitment and do not let self-doubt or negativity affect their actions once they have chosen a path. The more you act like this, the more people will respond positively to you and look to you for guidance.

One way of looking and sounding confident is to slow down your speech and actions. People who are insecure or panicking tend to speak more quickly and in a higher tone of voice. They seek approval from others by searching their faces instead of maintaining steady eye contact. They may also move in a disjointed, jerky way or use unconscious nervous gestures to try to calm themselves.

Confidence also comes from body language. Project your values and your strength with every movement of the body. Keep the chin up and the chest out. Make eye contact with the person you are talking to, and truly listen to what they are saying – ironically, studies have shown that a person who spends more time

A Confident Demeanour

A strong physical posture can have a great effect on your own feelings of confidence and authority. It also inspires confidence in those around you and is one of the leadership qualities deemed vital in the military. Even if you feel less than confident on the inside, act confident on the outside and your mood will soon improve.

A Leading Mentality

Military leaders need, above all, to make clear decisions, even in the most chaotic and destructive situations. In fact, most authorities say that, in combat, making no decision is actually worse than making a bad decision.

listening than speaking is judged to be more confident than someone who simply talks all the time. If you have to give orders, give them clearly and succinctly, and respond to any feedback honestly and intelligently.

Leadership

Studies into what makes a good leader have been underway in earnest since World War I, when the usual method of choosing officers from good families or schools was not yielding enough men to match the numbers falling in battle.

Taking on a leadership role may come naturally to some, while others need to work at it, but at some point in a military career most soldiers will have to rise to some level of leadership, even if just as a junior NCO. Those entering the armed services at officer level must quickly gain command of soldiers with more field time and experience than them, which is a significant challenge of character and ability.

The US military uses certain techniques for leadership that can be successfully applied to most areas of life. The reason for their success can be down to one very important point – if leaders make the wrong decision, or make no decision at all, lives will almost certainly be lost instead of saved. The pressure is immense, but so are the rewards.

Acting Under Pressure

The saying 'doing something is better than doing nothing' is well known. The principle of quick decision-making is vital for those in the elite forces, where you may have split seconds to reach a decision or form a plan, then act on it. In such situations, your plan does not have the temporal space to be perfect. For this reason the US Marine Corps has the concept of the '70 per cent solution'. It states that a plan designed for 100 per cent success is not only unrealistic but too slow to implement and, on the battlefield, the side that can dictate the highest operational tempo usually wins. For this reason, the Marine Corps have the 70 per cent solution, a plan that on balance is highly likely to succeed but which can be enacted *now*, with improvisational adjustments as it unfolds.

The 70 per cent solution might seem dangerous, but fast-moving, dangerous situations do not present the time to try to consider every detail before making a decision. Men and women could be waiting for your command before acting; every second could be costing lives. Training exercises will give you vital experience in making these quick decisions, but even activities such as football or softball (especially useful if there is an audience all giving opposing views on what to do) will help you to follow your instincts.

Once you have made your decision as leader, you need to be clear and concise about what is to be done. The essence of the plan means that people need to know the end outcome and what their role is, but they can figure out the details themselves. Empowering your team means that while you are leading them, they are also managing their own area of expertise. This was one of General Dwight D. Eisenhower's (1890–1969) leadership tools. He led by persuasion, not force, and enabled people to take ownership of their choices. As his memorable quotation reads: 'What counts is not necessarily the size of the dog in the fight – it's the size of the fight in the dog.'

Legitimate Authority

It is often thought that strong leadership comes hand-in-hand with authority. For Eisenhower and many other successful military leaders, flexibility and being able to react quickly to changing situations is vital in the armed forces. You may suddenly realize that the opposition have far greater firepower than was first thought, which means that your initial decision to attack would be a suicide mission. Prior planning for contingencies such as these, while it may never be able to cover every eventuality, can be vital in saving time in the field. Knowing your

Intelligence Test

8		
6		2

Total: 15

2		
		3

Use 2, 3, 4, 5, 6, 7, 8, 9, 10 Total: 18

In the example given to the right, the total is 12. This is the same whether the row is calculated horizontally, or vertically. Complete the boxes laid out below, following the same principles, but to the totals given underneath each of the boxes.

3	2	7
8	4	0
1	6	5

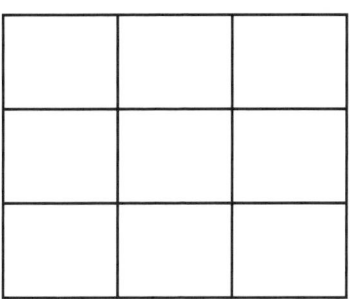

Total: 27

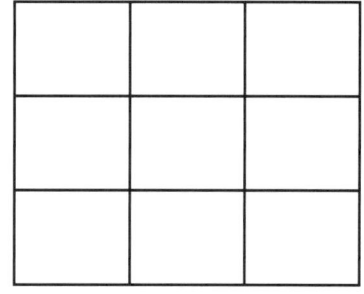

Total: 39

Use 4, 5, 6, 7, 8, 9, 10, 11, 12 Total: 24

Use 0, 5, 10, 15, 20, 25, 30, 35, 40 Total: 60

(See answers on page 308)

Tank Commander in Action

This map of a tank commander negotiating his way through obstacles highlights the importance of decision-making, earned during a combination of military training and combat experience.

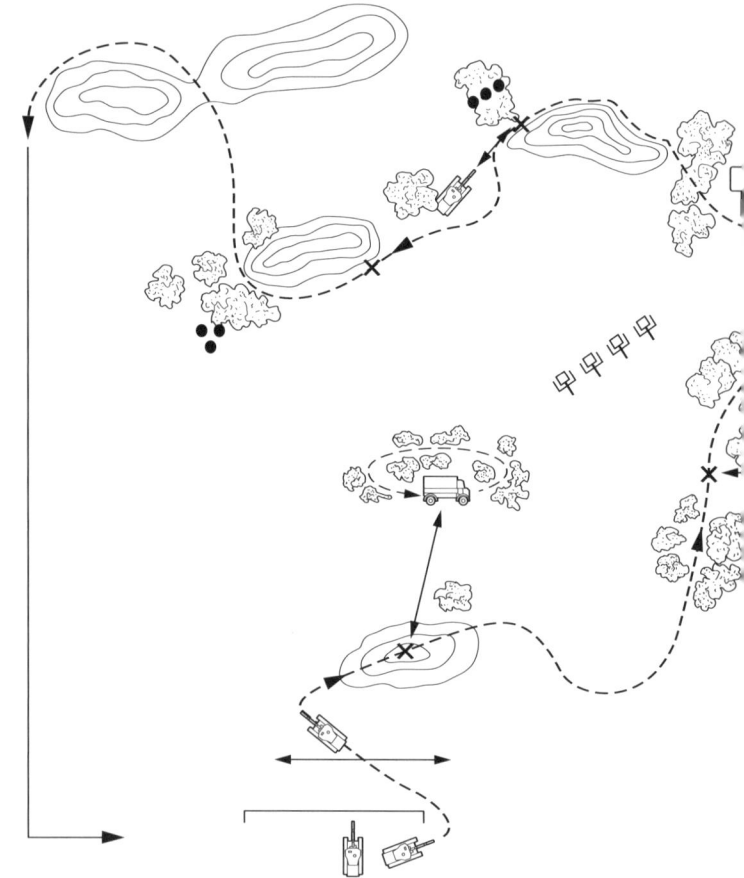

options and your strengths, be they your men, your equipment or your environment, makes your leadership decisions more judicious.

Planning and Knowledge

Officer training is made exceptionally demanding because the officer must eventually stand as a role model to the men beneath him. He must also demonstrate a formidable range of technical, logistical and operational knowledge, being able to plan an action without neglecting any essential element.

When it comes to operations, the true leader must control the processes of deployment and action from beginning to end. Planning and preparation for battle involves several key actions that must be directed towards using, in Clausewitz's words, 'physical force in order to compel the other to do his will'. Operational planning is a massive topic in its own right, and is covered in Chapter 5: Defeating the Opponent, but a common way in which officers are trained in planning and preparation is to use 'reverse planning'. As its name suggests, this process is based on defining the desired end result and then working backwards in time to fill in all the stages necessary to achieve that objective. Once you have worked back to the starting point, you have a complete plan for the mission.

Book Learning

Never overlook the importance of academic learning to tactical awareness. Generations of military experience is laid down in books, and spending time reading about these experiences gives you a shortcut to battlefield knowledge.

Tactical Training

Sand-table training is useful in developing decision-making and tactical skills. It is more visual than working on paper, allowing soldiers to imagine their position and actions.

One useful technique in the planning stage is what is known as 'rule of three thinking', as coined by the US Marine Corps and described in David Freedman's book *Corps Business: The 30 Management Principles of the US Marines* (New York, HarperCollins, 2000). In this logical leadership tool, the officer or soldier takes any complex situation he is facing and quickly produces three alternative courses of action.

Two courses of action provide insufficient or inflexible choice, and four courses too many options, which can lead to mental paralysis. Three choices, however, have been found to be optimal for making rapid, informed decisions. The officer must, with good reason yet possibly applying the 70 per cent solution ethos, select one of the choices and then run with it, seeking its success with maximum conviction and commitment.

We have now looked at a range of mental tools to help survival in military life. These techniques can result in a disciplined, resilient mind, prepared for battle. This mental state was poetically expressed by Chinese strategist Sun Tzu in the 5th century BCE. Sun Tzu's *The Art of War* has long held up as a definitive work of military strategy. His states clearly that mental endurance and self-knowledge can be powerful

US Army problem-solving process

1. Recognize and Define the Problem
2. Gather Facts and Make Assumptions
3. Define End States and Establish Criteria
4. Develop Possible Solutions
5. Analyze and Compare Possible Solutions
6. Select and Implement Solution
7. Analyze Solution for Effectiveness

weapons in their own right, and that winning the battle over the self is a precursor to winning the battle with the enemy:

'So it is said that if you know your enemies and know yourself, you can win a hundred battles without a single loss. If you only know yourself, but not your opponent, you may win or may lose. If you know neither yourself nor your enemy, you will always endanger yourself.'

Military training is unlike any other form of instruction in the civilian world. It has multiple purposes, from giving the recruit the ability to operate a modern assault rifle through to how to survive in the wild. If we were to pick a common theme running through training, however, it is to imbue the recruit with the military mind-set.

Soldiers, by their very profession, must think in ways that have few parallels in the civilian world. For example, they must be able to use violence purposefully towards achieving tactical goals, and they must be able to obey commands even if those commands put them in harm's way. They have to view what we might see as a beautiful landscape as *terrain*, full of tactical dangers and possibilities. Soldiers also need to acquire total conversancy with weapons that if owned in the civilian world might put them in prison for many years.

Above all, military training aims to breed warriors. Indeed, in 2003 the US Army established a Warrior Ethos Program aimed at establishing the core principles of the martial spirit

....

The military mindset extends to every area of the soldier's life. Even in simple matters, such as polishing boots, he or she should exhibit discipline, awareness and a sense of unit pride.

4

Training stands as the foundation of a soldier's mental endurance. A military training regime reshapes a civilian and changes the very way he or she looks at – and deals with – the world.

Training

Trusting the Team

The US military inculcates team-building skills from the outset, knowing that its soldiers are stronger as members of a united squad. Here, a servicewoman is able to walk a beam with her eyes closed, secure in the knowledge that her team mates are looking out for her and will catch her if she falls.

among its forces. One of the results of this programme was a modified version of the Soldier's Creed, a declaration shouted out by US soldiers when standing to attention and stating their fealty to army and country (see box).

When compared to the previous version of the Soldier's Creed, this declaration has a far greater emphasis on the profession of arms. It describes a single-minded individual, utterly confident in his combat skills and willing to engage in the blood and horror of 'close combat' to protect himself, his country and his comrades. Lines 4–6 also show an indefatigable commitment to the mission, placing personal desire beneath the obligation to get the job done. (Lines 4–7 are the main contribution to the creed from the Warrior Ethos Program.) At the same time, the warrior is a team player, totally committed to the welfare of the men in his unit, even to the extent of not leaving their bodies behind on the battlefield.

Other nations have similar creeds, or at least implement training programmes with similar values. Yet how do you take a man or woman off the street and reshape his or her mental fabric to match this unique set of values? In this chapter we will look at the various mental strategies and goals of military training.

US Soldier's Creed

In its new form, incorporating the Warrior Ethos codes, the creed reads as follows:
I am an American Soldier.
I am a Warrior and a member of a team.
I serve the people of the United States, and live the Army Values.
I will always place the mission first.
I will never accept defeat.
I will never quit.
I will never leave a fallen comrade.
I am disciplined, physically and mentally tough, trained and proficient in my warrior tasks and drills.
I always maintain my arms, my equipment and myself.
I am an expert and I am a professional.
I stand ready to deploy, engage and destroy the enemies of the United States of America in close combat.
I am a guardian of freedom and the American way of life.
I am an American Soldier.

Developing Discipline

Discipline is key to surviving both basic training and military life. Although it can be a harsh and often exhausting regime, its purpose is to foster soldiers who can retain clear thinking even under severe stress.

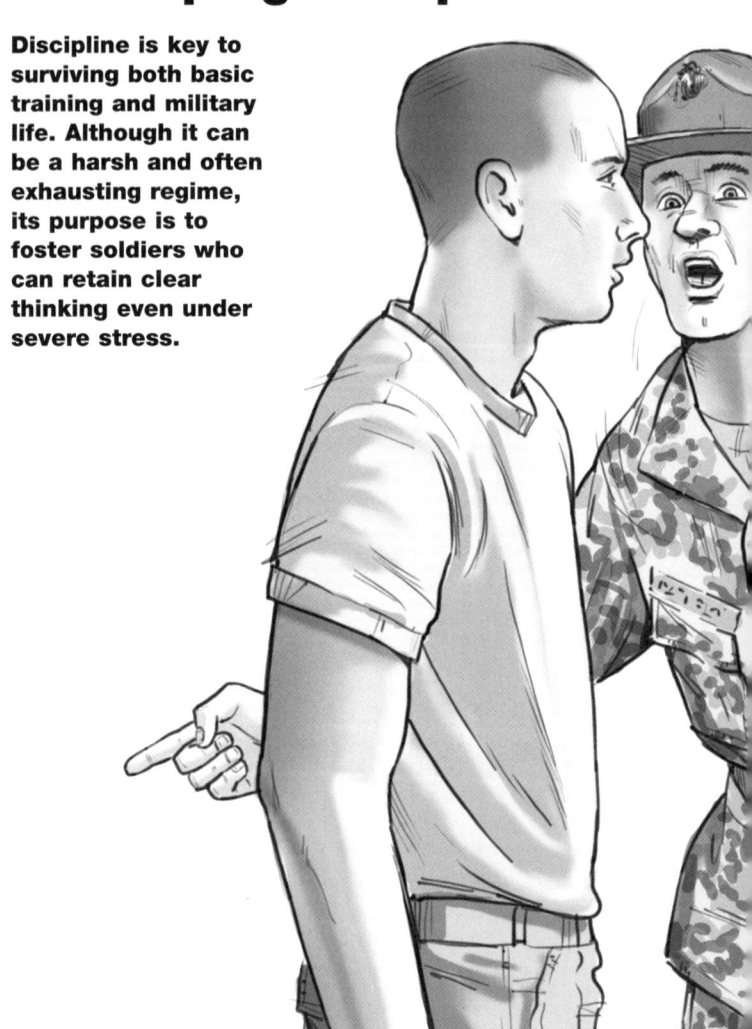

Discipline

One of the key objectives of military training is quite simply to inculcate the soldier with discipline to obey orders from superiors, even if those orders can put the soldier in direct danger. In today's less deferential age, getting young individuals to accept and embrace discipline within a hierarchical structure can be problematic.

One of the key reasons why drill instructors (DIs) tend to place such extreme demands on new recruits is to test their responses to discipline, in every context from making a bed in accordance with prescribed military standards to responding quickly to tactical directives. To the recruits, the DI's insistence on minute details of uniform presentation and etiquette might at first appear as pedantry, but the military understands that someone who is disciplined with the details will generally be more disciplined in high-pressure combat situations. They are looking for strong characters, ones who will throw themselves with commitment into whatever task they face.

Another key goal of military discipline is to foster a group-oriented mindset in an individual. In the basic training of many professional armies, the infractions of a single soldier can result in punishments for the entire squad or platoon. This position fosters team

Following Orders

Every order, no matter how small, must be followed to the letter during military training. Failure to achieve the high standards expected of soldiers may result in the whole unit being punished. Therefore, soldiers have an extra incentive to get things right.

Success in Battle

Every soldier, non-commissioned officer (NCO), warrant officer and officer has one primary mission – to be trained and ready to fight and win their nation's wars. Success in battle does not happen by accident; it is a direct result of tough, realistic and challenging training. The Army exists to deter war or, if deterrence fails, to re-establish peace through

victory in combat wherever US interests are challenged. To accomplish this, the Army's forces must be able to perform their assigned strategic, operational and tactical missions. For deterrence to be effective, potential enemies must know with certainty that the Army has the credible, demonstrable capability to mobilize, deploy, fight, sustain and win any conflict. Training is the process that melds human and materiel resources into these required capabilities. The Army has an obligation to the American people to ensure its soldiers go into battle with the assurance of success and survival. This is an obligation that only rigorous and realistic training, conducted to standard, can fulfil.

– US Army FM 7-0, *Training the Force* (22 October 2002)

responsibility – no man can shirk his duties without affecting his fellow recruits. The net effect of this system is that either a soldier drops out quickly from the training programme or he becomes committed to the welfare of his comrades – the latter being exactly the type of mental attitude the DIs want to see.

Training Regime

For the soldier adjusting to the world of military discipline, the experience can be brutal, especially when that discipline is delivered with high-pressure intensity by the DIs. The recruits are screamed at, dragged out of bed at all hours and forced to perform mind-numbing, exhausting routines, all while fulfilling orders to the letter. The situation for Special Forces recruits is even worse, especially when sleep deprivation is factored in. During the renowned US Army Ranger School training, for example, those undergoing training may well average just three or four hours of sleep a night for a period of several weeks. One effect of the sleep deprivation is a marked drop in cognitive function, making the soldier struggle to comprehend and remember even the simplest orders.

For any recruit, be it Special Forces or regular units, the extreme discipline of the training phase must be embraced rather than feared. The DIs are looking not only for people who can be externally disciplined, but also those who exhibit *self-discipline* – a mastery of themselves without necessarily requiring outside pressure to do what is right or required. Therefore, the self-aware recruit will not simply display a slavish adherence to orders, but at the same time demonstrate that he has taken the principles of discipline deep into his own character. The Drill Instructor's Creed of the US Marine Corps gives some insight into the DI mentality, and what he hopes the recruit will attain:

> *These recruits are entrusted to my care. I will train them to the best of my ability. I will develop them into smartly disciplined, physically fit, basically trained Marines, thoroughly indoctrinated in love of the Corps and country. I will demand of them and demonstrate by my own example the highest standards of personal conduct, morality and professional skill.*
> – US Marine Corps, Drill Instructor's Creed

The word 'indoctrinated' might, to many in the civilian world, be troubling, suggesting a sense of almost robotic programming. But, in truth, neither the Marine Corps nor most other progressive armies want automatons. The last sentence of the creed, however, gets more to

Competitive Spirit

Here, US military recruits race to be the first to complete an obstacle course. The task is important, as every recruit must complete the course to pass training. Yet, the best recruits will also ensure that their team-mates succeed as well as themselves, sometimes sacrificing coming first to help those who need assistance.

Route March

A demanding test of endurance, the route march involves recruits completing a long march carrying full pack and equipment. The pace modulates between a fast walk and a slow run, sapping energy over the hours.

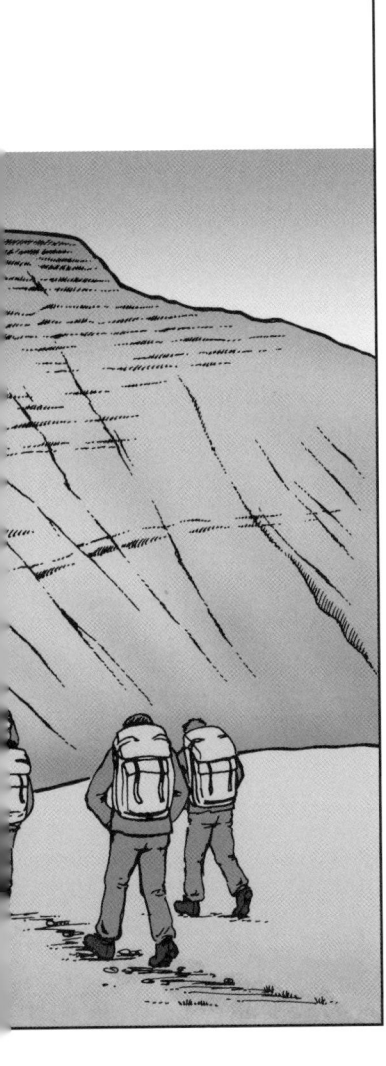

the heart of the issue, indicating that the DIs want to develop young men and women of high personal standards in every aspect of their lives.

In terms of practical advice for surviving the discipline of boot camp or any other training regime, the following tips come from soldiers who have been through the process:

- Never volunteer for anything, but fulfil every order to the highest possible standards.
- Remain focused during training – think about the most efficient way to complete an order.
- Unless ordered otherwise, help each other out when fulfilling duties. Make discipline a cooperative team effort.
- Show instant enthusiasm and commitment when given an order – any hesitancy or sulkiness will only result in further punishment.
- Regard training as a serious game – retain your sense of humour and keep your focus on the big picture (such as passing your training).
- Take each day as it comes, and do your best within that day.
- Make sure that you rest whenever you can.

Aggression

Aggression is not a popular word to use in today's society, as it carries with it implications of a mindless, violent individual with uncontrolled emotions. Such an individual would indeed scarcely be of any use to a modern army, as he would either get his comrades killed through rash actions or perpetrate the types of atrocity that can bring entire divisions into disrepute. What the military wants from its soldiers is controlled aggression – the ability to deliver focused violence against a defined enemy while also retaining an awareness of tactical and operational requirements. In situations where the soldiers are also acting as peacekeepers, they must be able to switch from violent action to reasoned negotiation within a matter of minutes – not an easy feat for many soldiers who have not yet left their teenage years.

One of the key features for building controlled aggression is unarmed combat training, which – depending on the unit and nationality – is delivered with varying degrees of brutality. The British Parachute Regiment puts its recruits through 'milling', during which a pair of recruits must box each other for one minute flat out. The purpose of the event is not to demonstrate fluid boxing skills, but to show evidence of a dogged aggression and toughness in the face of physical punishment; if the soldier wavers in his commitment to the fight, he may have to do it all over again.

In many other elite units, unarmed combat training incorporates random,

Milling

Milling is a form of courage testing practised by the Parachute Regiment and other elite formations. It consists of boxing flat out for one minute straight, with instructors looking for persistent courage rather than good boxing technique.

Unarmed Combat – Dirty Tricks

Poke in the eye

Knee to groin

Unarmed combat training is an exercise in controlled aggression. Both parts of the equation are required – the soldier must aim to destroy or incapacitate the enemy without compunction, but the actions need to be kept as clear and controlled as possible.

Groin grab

Groin grab-face push

unexpected attacks by instructors on recruits to test a soldier's mettle. In Soviet Spetsnaz Special Forces, this type of treatment – according to those who have been through it – borders on the life threatening. In some exercises, a single Spetsnaz recruit is attacked by multiple assailants and has to survive a session that frequently results in broken bones, bleeding and unconsciousness.

Western armies tend to shy away from such excesses, at least publicly, but brutality was part and parcel of training up until very recently. An article in *The Tuscaloosa News* on 8 January 1973 raised serious questions about the cruelties of training in the US Marine Corps:

> *We have gathered evidence that Marine recruits have been kicked and beaten and clubbed with rifle butts. They have been forced to clear floors with their tongues, stand naked for hours in front of full-length mirrors and submit to even worse indignities. Several recruits have told us that they were required to lie in bed at attention and pray for war.*
>
> *Spokesmen for the Marine Corps acknowledge that the training is rugged, but deny that it is barbaric or sadistic. 'The training must prepare a Marine to accomplish his mission under the most trying battlefield*

Focus Pad Drills

Focus pads are extremely versatile training tools. They can be used for knee and elbow strikes as well as punches. Kicks can also be trained, but not at full power. The pads can also be used in unusual or awkward situations, such as striking from the ground or at a downed opponent.

conditions, but it does not eradicate an individual's moral training or his human feelings,' said one.
– Jack Anderson,
'Marine Training Barbaric',
The Tuscaloosa News
(8 January 1973)

The report went on to reveal that in the previous five years the USMC had incurred 63 deaths during combat training, while the army – which had seven times as many recruits – took just 35 training deaths.

Many of the excesses of training have been ironed out in the Western world over the last two decades. (USMC DIs, for example, have largely moved away from their florid skill with profanities, as demonstrated in the opening sequence of Stanley's Kubrick's 1987 film *Full Metal Jacket*, with Senior DI Gunnery Sergeant Hartman, played brilliantly by actual former Marine DI Ronald Lee Emery.) Yet traditions of rough training die hard. In November 2005, in Britain, there was public outcry after a video showed Royal Marine

Commandos, stripped naked, fighting each other in some manner of initiation ceremony. At one point an NCO kicks another soldier in the face, knocking him unconscious.

Such behaviour is indeed unacceptable, but there is no doubt that soldiers need to be able to tap into extreme aggression on the battlefield, and for many this has to be instilled during training. Unarmed combat and punishing physical training goes some way to accomplishing this, as it teaches the soldier to commit his body

unreservedly to a purpose and drag an often unwilling mind along with it. The training also, quite unashamedly, teaches men (and sometimes women) to kill. Such is partly achieved through an appeal to logic – it is a simple truism that if a soldier does not kill his enemy, the enemy might well kill him or his comrades. Sometimes it is also achieved through patriotism, imbuing the idea that the act of killing can serve a greater purpose of protecting the soldier's country, or at least promoting a worthy way of life or set of values.

Fighting Mindset

Preparing a soldier so that he is ready to fight is a vital part of military training. Here, a soldier adopts a guard position, putting his body in the optimal position for an unarmed encounter. Such training instils confidence as well as fighting ability.

In some nations, and at certain times in history, soldiers have been indoctrinated in crude racial views that hold opponents as something less than fully human, hence their destruction does not warrant moral compunction. Egregious examples of this can be found in the worst excesses of the Nazi regime during World War II, when Eastern Europeans and Jews were classified as *Untermensch* (sub-humans), and so were slaughtered in their millions as part of Hitler's hideous attempt at racial engineering.

Thankfully, examples of such racial prejudice, at least at an official level, seem to be relatively rare in modern armies, although it is undoubted that many commanders still play on the idea of one nation's armed forces somehow being martially and spiritually superior to those of another nation. However, as the following chapter will explore in greater detail, it is not a natural act for human beings to kill, and to enable them to do so efficiently and with little compunction takes considerable psychological rewiring.

Training to Kill

A tested method of fostering the warrior spirit is to get the individual soldier to buy into the martial identity of the group. From the moment a recruit enters basic training, he is surrounded by a world of unified military values and a warrior outlook, an environment of weapons, uniforms, armoured vehicles, marching and tactics, plus a desire to be tested in conflict. (The civilian world often underestimates the young soldier's desire to fight a war; it is not uncommon to hear of soldiers crying with frustration when other units are deployed to combat zones but they are left behind at home.)

The net effect of this military world is that eventually soldiers identify themselves with the group values and martial traditions, putting on mental armour over their civilian values and enabling them to fight and kill with singular commitment. As psychologists have discovered, this is partly to do with 'group thinking', a recognized phenomenon when an individual subsumes his or her individual personality to the corporate personality. (Group thinking is one explanation for why seemingly well-balanced people might find themselves participating in riots.) The group-thinking propensity has to be controlled by officers, as it is a root ingredient of many wartime atrocities (see next chapter), but it undoubtedly serves a valuable purpose in getting individuals to overcome natural inhibitions and fight with commitment.

Another element of aggression training is, quite literally, to get the soldier to practise adopting a ferocious personality. A time-

Bayonet Training

While the bayonet is rarely used in modern warfare, being able to use it with aggression in training shows a will to attack and wound at close quarters, plus a determination to defeat the enemy. Trainers are looking for complete commitment to the attack – a desire to destroy rather than just stab the target.

The Spirit of the Bayonet

The will to meet and destroy the enemy in hand-to-hand combat is the spirit of the bayonet. It springs from the fighter's confidence, courage and grim determination, and is the result of vigorous training. Through training, the fighting instinct of the individual soldier is developed to the highest point. The will to use the bayonet first appears in the trainee when he begins to handle it with facility, and increases as his confidence grows. The full development of his physical prowess and complete confidence in his weapon culminates in the final expression of the spirit of the bayonet – fierce and relentless destruction of the enemy. For the enemy, demoralizing fear of the bayonet is added to the

destructive power of every bomb, shell, bullet and grenade that supports and precedes the bayonet attack.

– War Department, FM 23–25, *Bayonet* (7 September 1943) p.1

honoured way of doing this is through bayonet training. (In modern warfare, bayonet fighting almost never occurs; a notable exception took place on 14 May 2004, when soldiers of the Argyll and Sutherland Highlanders charged an Iraqi insurgent force in Al Amara, Iraq, killing about 28 of the enemy in ferocious hand-to-hand fighting.) The value of bayonet training, therefore, is not for its practical combat purpose but to foster the martial spirit and train the soldier to strip away his humanity temporarily and experience the sheer brutality required to kill another human being at close quarters. It also encourages the soldier to be willing to close with the enemy, without which terrain might not be secured.

Bayonet training typically consists of soldiers charging stuffed sacks (which may or may not be roughly human shaped), usually screaming dementedly while plunging the blade deep into the target. The DIs will encourage the men to imagine that the sack is their enemy, who they are pitilessly doing to death. The DIs are looking for men who can embrace the moment and show the capacity for focused violence.

Automatic Responses

One aspect of modern aggression training actually has little to do with emotion at all. This is the simple practice of repetition. Under

Stripping Down a Weapon

Having a detailed knowledge of his weapon, including how it works and how to maintain it, is critical for a soldier. Its maintenence and use should become second-nature, almost an extension of his own body.

The USMC Rifleman's Creed

This is my rifle. There are many like it, but this one is mine.

My rifle is my best friend. It is my life. I must master it as I must master my life.

My rifle, without me, is useless. Without my rifle, I am useless. I must fire my rifle true. I must shoot straighter than my enemy who is trying to kill me. I must shoot him before he shoots me. I will…

My rifle and myself know that what counts in this war is not the rounds we fire, the noise of our burst or the smoke we make. We know that it is the hits that count. We will hit…

My rifle is human, even as I, because it is my life. Thus, I will learn it as a brother. I will learn its weaknesses, its strength, its parts, its accessories, its sights and its barrel. I will keep my rifle clean and ready, even as I am clean and ready. We will become part of each other. We will…

Before God, I swear this creed. My rifle and myself are the defenders of my country. We are the masters of our enemy. We are the saviours of my life.

So be it, until victory is America's and there is no enemy, but peace!

tress, the mind tends to revert to instinctive, automatic reactions rather than those controlled by higher thought. Intensive, repetitive training might seem to be reworking old ground over and over, but what it achieves is to give the soldier a practical range of responses to combat, ones that are so ingrained he doesn't need to think about them to put them into action.

For example, it is vital that soldiers learn how to move quickly and safely between places of cover when under fire. A mantra sometimes used to help them do this is 'I'm up, I'm moving, he's seen me, down.' Said out loud with natural timing, this phrase guides the soldier as to how long he can stay exposed before an enemy spots him and takes a shot. If, during basic training, the soldier repeats and follows this instruction literally hundreds of times, then it will become a second-nature response in combat. With the rounds whizzing in, striking the ground and features around him, his training will, hopefully, 'take over' (a phase soldiers often used by soldiers about the relationship between combat and training) and give him sensible, automatic responses.

More offensively, the same principles can be applied to handling firearms. One way around the problems identified by official US Army historian S.L.A. Marshall is to train soldiers constantly in weapons handling, getting them to fire thousands of rounds in training at every possible presentation of target. The physical relationship between the soldier and the firearm becomes almost as natural and symbiotic as between the soldier and his own limbs. The act of putting the sights on a human-shaped figure and pulling the trigger becomes instinctive, meaning that now in combat almost every frontline soldier will fire his weapon in action, and accurately. The results can be astonishing. During the infamous 'Black Hawk Down' clash between several hundred US/UN forces (principally US Army Rangers) and thousands of Somali militia fighters in Mogadishu on 3–4 October 1993, the highly trained US forces took fewer than 100 casualties, while inflicting anywhere between 1500 and 3000 casualties on the poorly trained militia troops.

Defensive Position

Maintaining defensive positions for long periods is both a physical and mental challenge to a soldier, who has to remain focused and alert at all times through boredom and environmental pressures. Unit leaders should establish regular shift patterns, replacing sentries after a few hours at their post.

Realism in Training

Soldiers can be given any number of logical reasons to fight a war, but such reasons do not necessarily mean that when the soldier actually faces action he will be able to fight. The simple fact is that war is a sensory overload, and the massive

'fight or flight' response that it provokes in the human body can reduce the most motivated of soldiers to helplessness. A British soldier who deployed on the beaches of Normandy on D-Day, 6 June 1944, later remarked about his shock at how his sergeant – a fearsome and powerful individual back at camp in England – become catatonic and tearful when he was placed in combat in France, such was the shock of battle.

In the aftermath of World War II, many psychological studies were done to ascertain the difference

Realistic Assault Course

Current military training is much more realistic than in previous years. Studies from World War II have shown that the more tough and realistic the training, the more likely a soldier is to perform during live combat.

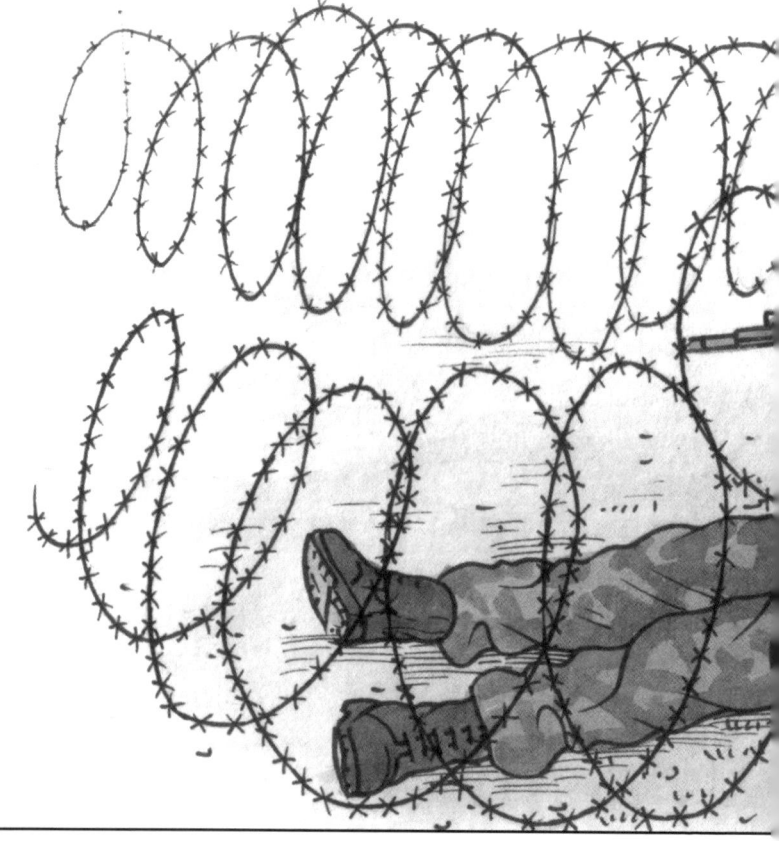

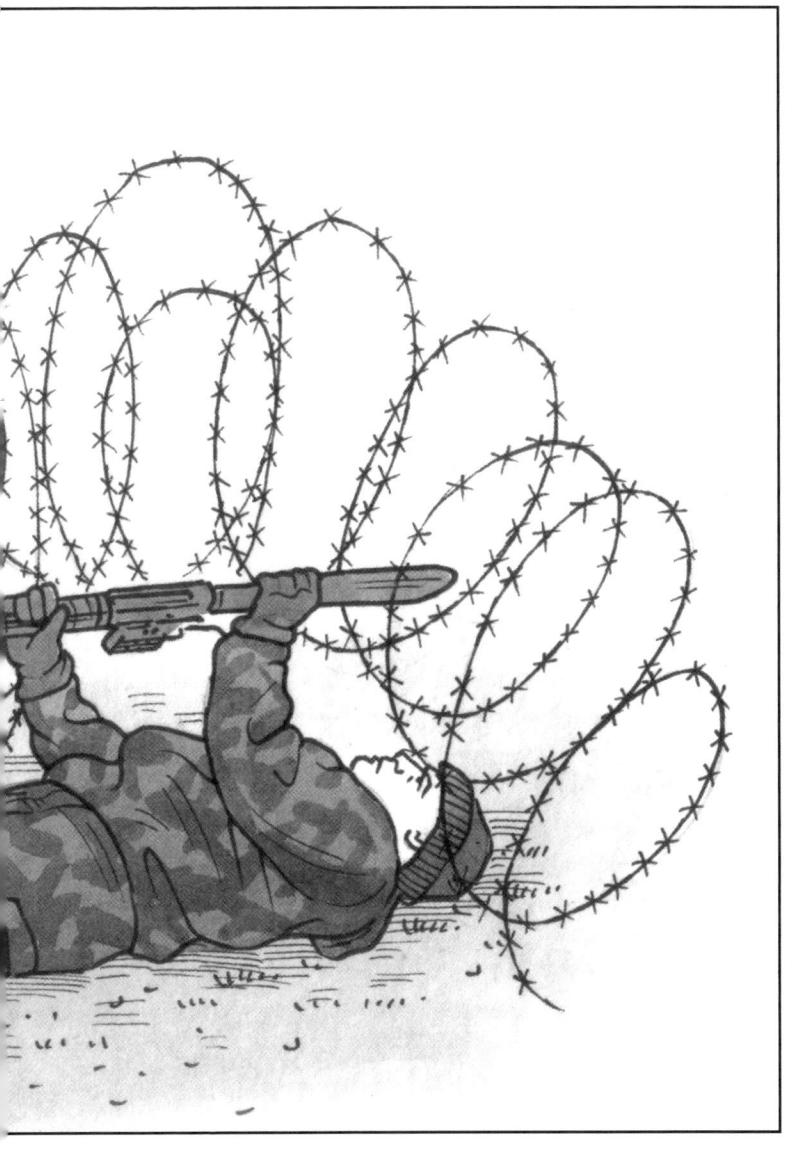

between those soldiers who would fight and those who would not. Some of the conclusions shocked the military establishment. S.L.A Marshall's book *Men Against Fire: The Problem of Battle Command* (1947) stated that during World War II only 15 per cent of Allied soldiers actually fired their weapons during combat. He found marked differences in the personalities of those prepared to fire their weapons (whom he termed 'fighters') and those who were not prepared to fire ('non-fighters'). Fighters usually opened fire from the start of the battle and kept firing throughout, compared to non-fighters who only opened fire in exceptional circumstances, if at all. Marshall continued his research in other contexts, most notably in Korea in 1950–53, where he found that more than 50 per cent of soldiers fired their weapons, partly due to the fact that leaders were more aware of the non-fighter issue and better prepared their men for action.

While inconsistencies and questions about Marshall's work continue, it remains an insightful and a relatively honest challenge to the notion that all soldiers are natural warriors. (We of course have to allow for the fact that the armies of World War II were predominantly composed of conscripts, not regular soldiers.) Marshall contested that 'fear of killing, rather than fear of being killed, was the most common cause of battle failure in the individual, and that fear of failure ran a close second.'

Mental Paralysis

During World War II and the postwar period, psychologists understood that the sheer strangeness and trauma of combat could lead to mental paralysis. Combat leaders therefore progressively realized that training could be reconfigured to provide some form of battle experience, without the dangers of combat itself. If training could be made as realistic as possible, it could provide a form of 'battle inoculation' (also known as 'battleproofing'), enabling soldiers to become familiar with the stresses of combat in a safe environment, so that they were still able to function when they came into contact with real action. Not only would battle inoculation make soldiers more efficient in combat, it would also give protection against post-traumatic stress disorder (PTSD).

As briefly discussed in Chapter 3, the human mind is essentially like an enormous filing system. When a person comes upon a new experience, that experience is compared to the 'files' of previous experience to see if there is already a guide to action. Depending on the relevance of the match, the individual is able to make a judgement and

Training Realism

Here a military recruit undergoes minefield clearance as part of his training. Such tests are often conducted with added stressors, such as nearby explosions, constant shouted instructions and harsh penalties for mistakes.

respond to the situation. If there is little previous experience, the brain finds the nearest equivalent and then makes a new file based on what happens. The problem with combat is that it is so extreme by nature that unless you have actually experienced it, there at first appears to be little you can do to prepare for it.

This is where battle inoculation can be used. The essence of battle inoculation is to make combat training as realistic as humanly possible without actually killing or injuring people. Basic forms of battle inoculation training in World War II consisted of getting soldiers to crawl on their bellies under barbed wire while live machine-gun fire cut the air above their heads. Thunderflashes detonating around them added to the sensation – albeit a pale imitation – of shellfire explosions. The US Marine Corps would add an extra ingredient of realism by strewing the earth with offal and pieces of raw meat to add an extra gore factor.

Simulated Combat

Note that a key ingredient of battle inoculation might be to place the soldier in the presence of genuine danger, such as the bullets flying inches above his head, as it is only when the danger is real that the soldier can become accustomed to dealing with the adrenalin response. This principle is seen in later SAS hostage-rescue training

Combat Mindset

Realistic training and battle inoculation mean that today's soldiers are far more likely to fire their weapons. By repeatedly doing so during training, the process becomes much more automatic so that, in times of stress, the reflexes take over.

Spetsnaz Equipment

Spetsnaz equipment includes an anti-tank missile, grenades, a sniper rifle, communications equiment, mines and rations. The soldier needs excellent organizational skills and technical awareness to deploy the right equipment correctly.

in the 'killing house', a special live-fire environment designed to replicate the interior of a building. In one exercise, a 'hostage' – an unarmed SAS soldier – is positioned surrounded by life-size cut-out figures of his terrorist captors. With incredible speed, an SAS team then makes an explosive entry using stun grenades – which impart a huge flash and bang but which have almost no lethality. The noise and smoke are intense and the room is plunged into darkness. In this confusion, the entry team target the terrorist figures with close-range bursts from MP5 submachine guns, the bullets cutting the air close around the SAS 'hostage', who must remain motionless if he is to stay alive. For all participating, the exercise is about as real as an experience of combat can be without the actual loss of human life.

Battle inoculation training has now risen to a level of realism unthinkable even 20 years ago. In the United States, private companies provide mock-up training environments for soldiers that almost exactly mirror the current theatres to which troops are likely to be deployed. The soldiers have to deal with locals speaking their native language (played by ethnic actors) and move around buildings and villages painstakingly constructed to replicate foreign dwellings both inside and out.

In simulated combat, powerful and stunning detonations erupt without warning to simulate IEDs, and rockets streak across the battlespace to represent RPGs. The 'opposing force' (OPFOR) will only use weapons available to the actual enemy in the field, such as the AK47, and both sides will fire either blanks or 'simunitions'. The blanks are allied to laser sensors on the firearms and on the soldier's uniform, indicating clearly when a soldier has been hit, and where. The simunitions, by contrast, are actual munitions that have an accurate ballistic performance of about 50m (164ft). When they hit a target, they not only leave a visible paint mark, they can also hurt, leaving substantial bruising. This minor wounding effect adds to the adrenalin of the combat simulation, furthering the battle inoculation effect.

Ultra-realism

The development of increasingly convincing theatrical make-up in recent years has also allowed battle inoculation companies to confront soldiers with horrifying combat wounds, ranging from gunshot to full amputations (amputees are often enlisted as actors to make the latter especially convincing). Furthermore, the use of 'cut-suits' – full-body outfits that can be opened up in surgical procedures, revealing authentic-looking innards – have

Urban Warfare

Urban warfare can be the ultimate example of conflict at its most chaotic. You may be confronted with hostile military enemy forces who have the advantage of knowing the terrain and environment far better than you. In addition, you may have to factor in the possibility of inflicting civilian casualties, or the moral complexities of separating friend from foe. Good communications and firm rules of engagement are useful in helping to decide when to engage.

Room Assault

A Special Forces counter-terrorist team conduct a room assault, detonating a stun grenade before making an aggressive entry. Constant practice inculcates the speed required for such an assault.

Rapid Reactions

The ability to distinguish between hostile and civilian targets, while in a rapid-fire exercise, is an excellent way of developing quick reactions. The aim is to make shooting an instinctive practice.

allowed combat medics to practise their field medicine training in ultra-realistic detail.

For a soldier to get the most out of battle inoculation training, he must throw himself imaginatively into the exercises without restraint, not doing anything to break the illusion of reality. By committing to the fiction wholeheartedly, he will prepare himself mentally for what he might encounter in battle and will dramatically improve his chances of survival.

Commitment

Gentlemen: you have now reached the last point. If anyone of you doesn't mean business let him say so now. An hour from now will be too late to back out. Once in, you've got to see it through. You've got to perform without flinching whatever duty is assigned you, regardless of the difficulty or the danger attending it. If it is garrison duty, you must attend to it. If it is meeting fever, you must be willing. If it is the closest kind of fighting, anxious for it. You must know how to ride, how to shoot, how to live in the open. Absolute obedience to every command is your first lesson. No matter what comes you mustn't squeal. Think it over – all of you. If any man wishes to withdraw he will be gladly excused, for others are ready to take his place.

– Theodore Roosevelt, 'Remarks to Recruits', 1898

The Ethical Warrior

There is an essential paradox at the heart of military training. At the same time as training soldiers to kill and use extreme violence, the military also wants men and women who are capable of enormous restraint, cultural sensitivity and even compassion.

Soldiers who do not have these qualities are likely to alienate the local population and force more recruits into enemy hands. More darkly, soldiers who strip empathy from their mental make-up are at greater risk of committing the atrocities that can cast dark shadows across an entire campaign. For such reasons, good military training will also foster an ethical attitude among its troops, promoting the values and standards that enable soldiers to act as ambassadors for their country or cause.

The British Army has in recent years given much thought to the concepts of values and standards, codifying them and issuing directives for how they can be distributed through the soldiery. Its *Values and Standards of the British Army* (2008) document states clearly that moral guidance is about both warfighting and peacemaking:

> The Army's Values and Standards are not abstract concepts whose origins lie solely in the demands of battle. Values are the moral

principles – the intangible character and spirit – that should guide and develop us into the sort of people we should be; whereas Standards are the authoritative yardsticks that define how we behave and on which we judge and measure that behaviour. They reflect, and are consistent with, the moral virtues and ethical principles that underpin any decent society. It is important that they are explained within that wider context, for it is vital that soldiers understand these Values and Standards and are able to apply them in today's complex operations. To that end, the articulation of these Values and Standards needs to be accompanied by a continuous and appropriate example by all commanders, junior and senior alike. Our Values and Standards apply at all times: whether on operations, in barracks, in our homes or off duty.

– British Army, *Values and Standards of the British Army* (2008)

Protecting Civilians

Here, US soldiers shield civilians with their own bodies, defending them from attack, demonstrating the ultimate commitment to their country and corps, and the values they represent.

The passage above defines values and standards as mutually interacting elements of the army, the standards being the concrete behavioural rules that demonstrate the values of the soldiery. One of the critical points to emerge from the statement is that the role of leaders is paramount in spreading standards and values, by their setting a 'continuous and appropriate example'. Indeed, as the next chapter will reflect upon, a common ingredient in many instances of atrocity is weak leadership. If soldiers see leaders showing the very best of the military character, then they are more likely to emulate and aspire to that example. Much like a business in the civilian world, military units have a corporate character that starts from the top and filters down through the ranks.

If we were to look for an example of this type of leadership in action we could go few places better than Kuwait on 19 March 2003, when Lieutenant Colonel Tim Collins of the 1st Battalion, Royal Irish Regiment, British Army, gave a speech to his men on the eve of the invasion of Iraq. His speech became famous for its martial attitude but also its essential humanity, as is evident in the following extract:

The enemy should be in no doubt that we are his nemesis and that we are bringing about his rightful destruction. There are many regional commanders who have stains on their souls and they are stoking the fires of hell for Saddam. He and his forces will be destroyed by this coalition for what they have done. As they die they will know their deeds have brought them to this place. Show them no pity.

It is a big step to take another human life. It is not to be done lightly. I know of men who have taken life needlessly in other conflicts, I can assure you they live with the Mark of Cain upon them. If someone surrenders to you then remember they have that right in international law and ensure that one day they go home to their family.

The ones who wish to fight, well, we aim to please.

If you harm the regiment or its history by over-enthusiasm in killing or in cowardice, know it is your family who will suffer. You will be shunned unless your conduct is of the highest for your deeds will follow you down through history. We will bring shame on neither our uniform or our nation.

The powerful heart of this extract is Collins' warning against needless violence. He emphasizes this point not merely from a moral perspective but also from a psychological one – those who overstep the mark can be haunted by their actions, socially and mentally, for the rest of their lives.

Military Virtues

The military virtues are not in a class apart; 'they are virtues which are virtues in every walk of life ... none the less virtues for being jewels set in blood and iron.' They include such qualities as courage, fortitude and loyalty. What is important about such qualities as these ... is that they acquire in the military context, in addition to their moral significance, a functional significance as well. The essential function of an armed force is to fight in battle. Given equally advanced military techniques, a force in which the qualities I have mentioned are more highly developed will usually defeat a stronger force in which they are less. Thus while you may indeed hope to meet these virtues in every walk of life and a good deal of educational effort is spent on developing them as being generally desirable, in the profession of arms they are functionally indispensable. The training, group organizations, the whole pattern of life of the professional man at arms is designed in a deliberate effort to foster them, not just because they are morally desirable in themselves, but because they contribute to military efficiency.

Lt Gen Sir John Hackett, 'The Profession of Arms', The 1962 Lees Knowles lectures

Furthermore, such actions can bring shame to the soldier's family and to his unit. The message of restraint is, however, balanced with an acknowledgement that the soldier will also need to fight when necessary. The implication is that those who require mercy will receive it, while those who resist will be destroyed.

The *Values and Standards of the British Army* goes on to list the qualities required under each category. To abbreviate:

Values
    Selfless commitment
    Courage
    Discipline
    Integrity
    Loyalty
    Respect for others

Treatment of Prisoners

When dealing with prisoners, soldiers often have to struggle with the fact that the prisoners were, just moments ago, an enemy who might have been trying to kill them. Officers need to take firm control when emotions are still running high, and should give clear procedural instructions to every soldier in the unit.

Standards
Lawful
Appropriate behaviour
Total professionalism
Application (applying the values and
   standards through training,
   leadership, etc)
The Service Test (the possibility of
   disciplinary action)

The codes here are similar to those expressed by the leadership of many other professional armies. Like all life philosophies, they must be practised on a daily basis if they are to become real in the experience of an individual soldier. The benefits of following such codes are that the soldier can place the need for violent action in a greater context, and retain the essential nobility of the profession of arms. Each soldier

must believe the values and standards on principle, not simply on fear of punishment, as the British Army document makes clear: 'Where the "bottom line" is not profit and loss, but the death or maiming of people including comrades, all soldiers must understand why they have to behave in a particular way, rather than following a set of rules blindly. Although Values and Standards can be imposed and regulated through discipline, it is self-discipline that will encourage all ranks to adhere to the Values and Standards, recognizing the inherent value of such qualities and conduct.' Developing such mature and circumspect individuals is the goal of all good military training and should be the continuing experience throughout a military career.

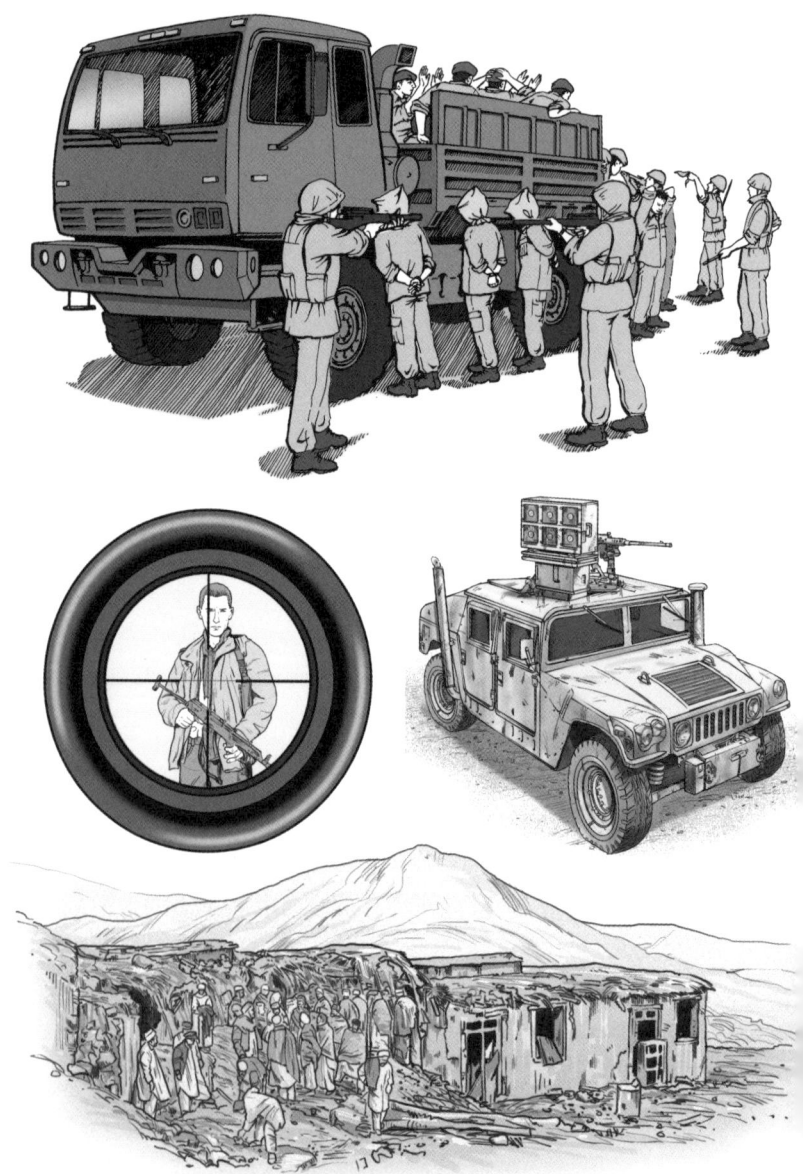

Combat is undoubtedly one of the greatest emotional challenges that a human being can face. In the presence of death and the violent sensations of war, a soldier has to stay focused on the mission outcome or survival, rather than simply shut down mentally in the face of extreme pressures.

Contrary to the way many Hollywood movies represent war, combat itself can be an incredibly chaotic experience. One of the best studies of this phenomenon, and of the practice of combat in general, is the short book entitled *Warfighting* by General A.M. Gray, Commandant of the Marine Corps between 1987 and 1991. *Warfighting* is a reflective work on both the nature of the battlefield and the issues armies face in defeating an opponent. A key concept that recurs throughout the book is that of 'friction', a combination of inertia and confusion produced by the battle between opposing sides. Gray defines friction as follows:

> *So portrayed, war appears a simple enterprise. But in practice, because of the*

. . . .

Soldiers operate in a world of threat. They must adjust to this fact quickly, and not let their imagination get the better of them in dangerous places.

5

In combat situations, the soldier needs to stay mentally sharp, even as the effects of adrenalin threaten to take over.

Defeating the Opponent

Combat Focus

Combat focus comes from having a clear sense of mission. Officers and NCOs should leave the soldier with no doubt as to his objective, while the individual soldier needs to take responsibility for meeting his part of the mission.

countless factors that impinge on it, the conduct of war becomes extremely difficult. These factors collectively have been called friction, which Clausewitz described as 'the force that makes the apparently easy so difficult'. Friction is the force that resists all action. It makes the simple difficult and the difficult seemingly impossible.

The very essence of war as a clash between opposed wills creates friction. It is critical to keep in mind that the enemy is not an inanimate object but an independent and animate force. The enemy seeks to resist our will and impose his own will on us. It is the dynamic interplay between his will and ours that makes war difficult and complex. In this environment, friction abounds.

– MCDP 1, Warfighting, page 5

Gray's point about the 'independent and animate' enemy is crucial. As combat has such high stakes, the enemy will typically use all his resources, technology, firepower, intelligence and spirit to defy your attempts to subjugate him. In such an environment, clear thinking and emotional control can make all the difference between victory and defeat, especially if you can impose confusion and mental disorder on the opponent.

How to deal with the friction of combat is the theme of this chapter. More specifically, we will look at the psychological aspects of combat, from self-control to controlling the enemy's responses to your actions. More darkly, this chapter will consider what it takes to kill someone, how to cope with that demand and how to prevent authorized killing tipping over into atrocity and inhumanity.

Finding Courage

Almost all soldiers, no matter how professional, will admit to being frightened by the prospect of combat, even if they are also excited by the possibility. (The indomitable US Army Commander General H. Norman Schwarzkopf once remarked: 'I've been scared in every war I've ever been in.') The fear is typically a legitimate combination of anxiety about being killed or wounded, with the added concern of mental breakdown resulting in the soldier letting his comrades down or, even worse, getting some of them killed.

Fear, as we note in other contexts in this book (see Chapter 7), can have a profound effect on a soldier's ability to operate. For a start, fear delivers a range of physiological changes that can be detrimental to the soldier's awareness of his surroundings and his ability to judge a situation clearly. In the context of a battle, fear's greatest threat is that it allows an opponent to dictate the tempo and development

Courage Through Action

Courage is often found not through willpower, but through simple action. Here, a soldier forces himself to stand up and throw a grenade, breaking his mental paralysis.

Physiological Effects of Fear

Body control The soldier can literally lose control of his bladder or bowels. Physical shaking – a natural response to fear – can interfere with fine motor control over limbs; this in turn can have serious implications if the soldier's survival depends on successfully operating a complex piece of weaponry or equipment.

Vision Under extreme fear a soldier can lose much of his peripheral vision and depth perception; the brain creates a 'tunnel vision' effect that focuses on the most immediate threat. This limited range of vision means that the soldier may be unaware of emerging dangers.

Hearing Fear can make hearing seem muted or distant, resulting in difficulty in comprehending orders or radio communications. In some instances the hearing might appear to shut down altogether. Problems with hearing are often exacerbated by the noise effects of gunfire and explosions.

Thinking Fear drains blood away from the frontal, rational parts of the brain, making reasoned thought difficult. It can also have the effect of slowing down the perception of time.

of the action. Fear, as any military commander will tell you, is also highly contagious – the sight of one man crumbling under pressure is likely to trigger sympathetic reactions in those around him, hence serious psychiatric casualties are usually removed from the battlefield extremely quickly before they have a wider effect on morale.

Major-General J.F.C. Fuller, one of Britain's more influential twentieth century military theorists, outlined the principles of fear acutely in his work *The Foundations of the Science of War* (1926). In it he states that 'Fear unhinges the will, and by unhinging the will it paralyses the reason; thoughts are dispersed in all direction in place of being concentrated on one definite aim.' The mental scattering that fear induces is a distinct threat in a combat situation, and even in an entire campaign.

Delivering Orders

A US Army unit comes under fire in Afghanistan. The soldier in the foreground issues brisk orders to those around him. Such clear-thinking individuals can make the difference between victory and defeat in action. When giving commands, they need to speak in clear, concise sentences that leave no room for misunderstanding. Nothing they say must be left open to interpretation.

Following a period of rising political and military tension in Afghanistan in January 1842, the elderly Major-General William Elphinstone led an East India Company army of 4500 soldiers and up to 12,000 camp followers (spouses, servants, children, etc.) out of Kabul, intending to make a journey of 140km (90 miles) to the safety of Jalalabad. The march was ill conceived in the first place, but during the journey itself – conducted through horrible mountainous winter conditions – fear and disorder took hold as Afghan tribal warriors launched constant ambushes and predatory attacks. The British cohesion fell apart under weak leadership, resulting in desertions, massacres and suicides. Fear, as much as the military situation, was the undoing of the column. In total more than 16,000 people were killed by the Afghans, and the sole individual to reach Jalalabad was one Surgeon William Brydon. He rode into the British base there on a dying horse and with part of his skull sheared off by a sword blow, and when asked where was the army he said weakly: 'I am the army.'

History is replete with examples of what occurs in battle when fear takes hold, producing routs and disorder among even veteran troops. Yet Fuller goes on to acknowledge that fear has a useful function, and there are ways in which it can be managed:

Fear, again, protects the body; it is the barometer of danger; is danger falling or rising, is it potent or weak? Fear should answer those questions, especially physical fear, and, thus knowing that danger confronts us, we can secure ourselves against it. Whilst moral fear is largely overcome by courage based on reason, physical fear is overcome by courage based on physical means.

– Fuller, The Foundations of the Science of War, 1926

Fuller raises the important point that fear has its purpose, alerting us to legitimate dangers to which we need to respond. The challenge, therefore, is to use the physical power that can come with fear alongside the ability to think rationally under stressful circumstances, and to do so better than your opponent. In essence, Fuller suggests that the most dangerous opponents in any battle are those within us.

Understanding Courage

Before we turn to look at how to use psychological principles to defeat external opponents, we will clarify techniques for handling such inner opponents. Many of these techniques are touched on in Chapter 3, but we can expand on this further in specific regard to courage. The ability to tap

Trauma in Combat

Seeing and experiencing trauma can cause a sensory overload – this soldier has temporarily lost control of his physical and mental faculties. While in such a state, he requires as much support as a physically wounded individual, and should be removed from the battlefield promptly.

into courage is vital. There is a common misunderstanding that people who are courageous tend to lack fear or a sense of self-preservation. Such individuals are actually, and thankfully, quite rare – those who don't fear might put others into dangerous situations. In fact, courage is rather the capacity to keep functioning even under the effects of fear.

In 1917, Major C.A. Bach of the US Army gave a speech to student officers at the Second Training Camp at Fort Sheridan, Illinois. A key passage dealt with the issue of courage:

> *Courage, however, is that firmness of spirit, that moral backbone, which, while fully appreciating the danger involved, nevertheless goes on with the understanding. Bravery is physical; courage is mental and moral. You may be cold all over; your hands may tremble; your legs may quake; your knees be ready to give way – that is fear. If, nevertheless, you go forward; if in spite of this physical defection you continue to lead your men against the enemy, you have courage.*
> – Major C.A. Bach, 1917

Bach observes that courage is not the absence of fear, but almost ignoring its effects through having an

Maintaining Focus

Mental training such as meditation and visualization can help you block out any negative thoughts or distractions when it counts. This soldier is completely focused on his objective, displaying total mental control, despite the fear he must be experiencing. His gaze is steady, his grip is solid and his balance is secure.

Team Motivation

Training as a team enables you to discover each other's strengths and use them positively. Team members can be encouraged and motivated by the fact that they are fighting for the good of the whole team, not just themselves. Unit cohesion also comes from the common distribution of tactical knowledge, and its regular practice in field exercises.

understanding of a higher purpose. Each soldier tends to find his own means of doing this, but the following are some common techniques:

- Make sure that you train hard and realistically (as noted in the previous chapter); doing this will provide you with a 'stress inoculation' against the effects of combat.
- Ensure that you have a crystal clear understanding of your orders. Under combat conditions, break down your overall mission

overwhelmed by the bigger picture.

- Get motivated as a team. Even though everyone in a unit might be afraid, collectively you can have confidence in your own abilities, and that alone can deliver courage. Speak confidently and clearly and hold your body in a way that projects resolve even if you do this artificially, like an actor. Doing this will not only make you feel more courageous, it will also encourage others to feel the same way.

- Have faith in yourself and your team. You are highly trained soldiers, so acknowledge that fact and show the enemy what you can do.

- Let negative thoughts come and go. Much in our imagination is uncontrollable, so try not to let disturbing mental visions affect you too much. Observe them without ascribing them too much significance and let them pass.

- Just do it. Throw yourself into the experience of combat. The more that you keep pushing yourself to accomplish objectives, the more your confidence under combat will increase. (Don't let yourself become overconfident, however – soldiers often observe that new recruits and seasoned veterans are frequently the people who are the most likely to become casualties.)

objective into small individually manageable chunks of information, such as reaching a piece of cover or laying down suppressive fire, and then concentrate all your efforts on performing each task in turn rather than being

Exploiting the Enemy's Needs

'If we are to win, we must be able to operate in a disorderly environment. In fact, we must not only be able to fight effectively in the face of disorder, we should seek to generate disorder for our opponent and use it as a weapon against him' (Gray, *Warfighting*, p.12). Much of the *Warfighting* manual is devoted to ways in which an army can dictate terms on the battlefield, not least through ways of controlling the enemy's mental state. Achieving mental dominance over an army means that physical dominance often follows, but it requires a good understanding of who the enemy is and what is important to him.

One route into this subject is the famous psychological structure known as 'Maslow's hierarchy of needs', posited by Abraham Maslow in his 1943 paper 'A Theory of Human Motivation'. Maslow defined human needs as a hierarchical structure, with the most basic physiological requirements at the bottom (breathing, sex, sleep, etc.) and the highest functions (creativity, reasoning, morality, etc.) at the top. The hierarchy is typically represented as a pyramid (see the illustration on page 180), although Maslow himself didn't present it like this. However, the needs have been arranged into five fundamental categories, in ascending order.

Squad Attack

Despite the noise and shock of the explosions behind them, none of these soldiers falters or looks back. They maintain what the Marine Corps terms 'tempo', a pace of operational movement that overwhelms the enemy.

Hierarchy of Needs

Maslow's hierarchy describes human needs in order of importance. This knowledge can be used to undermine and defeat your enemy.

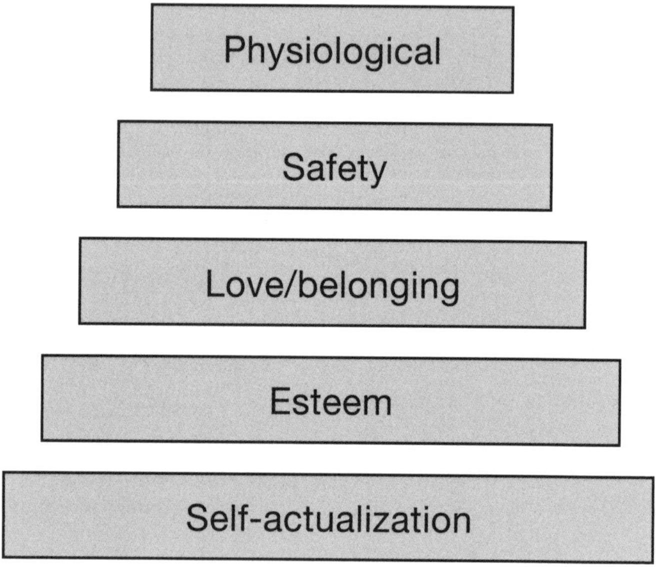

Physiological

Safety

Love/belonging

Esteem

Self-actualization

In a military context, there is value to understanding these needs. Undermine the foundations on which they rest and you can hopefully bring about the collapse of the enemy's unit cohesion. The means of hacking away at these foundations are multiple and range from subtle psychological operations through to outright and massive violence.

Physiological Needs
Physiological needs are the most essential functions of the human body – breathing, food, water,

excretion, sleep, sex, and so on. On the most obvious level, the most immediate way for an army to interfere with the enemy's physiological processes is through firepower – killing or wounding the opposing soldiers. Yet there are other routes to destabilizing the physical dependencies of an opposing force.

If the enemy's supply system can be threatened – by raids, encirclement, long-range shelling or aerial bombing – then you can literally impose restrictions upon

Undermining the Enemy

Understanding what makes you feel fear or become demotivated is a valuable lesson, as it is likely that your enemy will experience similar feelings. Removing access to basic needs can result in an enemy that is more compliant and easier to dominate.

their nutrition, diet and health. This practice was expressed most conspicuously during the sieges of fortifications in the medieval period; these actions were basically competitions to see whose physiological needs cracked first. At Henry V's siege of Harfleur in August to September 1415, for example, the month-long siege by the British troops compelled the town's commanders to surrender as starvation took hold. It was a close-run thing, however – Henry's men found their own physiological state weakened by insanitary living conditions, which resulted in dysentery (or the 'bloody flux' as it was known then) killing or incapacitating hundreds of men.

Logistical warfare is now recognized as one of the most critical components in defeating an enemy. Much of the success of Hitler's *Blitzkrieg* tactics in World War II was due to rapid incursions against enemy supply lines. The French Maginot Line defences, for example, were first bypassed and then encircled in German operations in France in June–July 1940. As a result, only 10 of the 50-plus major emplacements were actually defeated in combat actions; the majority were simply obliged to surrender when they were cut off from the rest of the French Army and the promise of resupply. During the battle of Singapore in February 1942,

one of the main reasons for the collapse of the British resistance was the Japanese capture of the island's main water supplies. (Given the short period of time people can survive without water, any military action to control water supplies can pay quick dividends.) In the postwar world, the United States suffered from serious issues consolidating remote jungle territories in Vietnam, because keeping troops stationed there permanently was simply too problematic in terms of logistics and manpower. The same is proving true today in Afghanistan.

Another basic need that can be targeted effectively is sleep. By keeping the enemy under constant pressure or disruption – such as through sporadic night-time shelling or frequent raids – his sleep patterns are necessarily interrupted. We have already noted the effects of sleep deprivation, and an enemy who is sleep deprived is likely to suffer from a decline in health, morale and tactical thinking. It is no coincidence that loud heavy metal music has been used in psychological warfare operations ('psyops') by US and other forces against the defenders of a fixed position; 10 days of rock music was applied by US psyops units in 1998 to flush Manuel Noriega, the military governor of Panama, out from his hiding place in the embassy of the Holy See. Such music has also been used in sleep

Targeting Sleep – Night Raids

Here night-time artillery fire is used to hit the enemy during his most vulnerable hours. As World War II demonstrated, continual shellfire can be an excellent tool for disorientating and weakening even the most resilient enemy over a matter of days.

deprivation torture of prisoners, showing how horribly effective it can be in breaking the will to resist.

The important point about attacking basic needs is not only that it can kill the enemy, but also that it can destabilize all other needs above the physiological level. For example, a person suffering from serious hunger is unlikely to have a good sense of self-esteem as the condition of his health deteriorates. Such are the cruel realities of war, but they are ones that can be exploited to bring a battle to an end.

Safety

Safety is intimately connected to physiological needs, but is really more about the perception of safety,

US Psyops

The mission of PSYOP is to influence the behavior of foreign target audiences (TAs) to support US national objectives. PSYOP accomplish this by conveying selected information and/or advising on actions that influence the emotions, motives, objective reasoning and ultimately the behavior of foreign audiences. Behavioral change is at the root of the PSYOP mission. Although concerned with the mental processes of the TA, it is the observable modification of TA behavior that determines the mission success of PSYOP. It is this link between influence and behavior that distinguishes PSYOP from other capabilities and activities of information operations (IO) and sets it apart as a unique core capability.

1-6. As a core capability of IO, PSYOP are considered primarily to be shaping operations that create and preserve opportunities for decisive operations. PSYOP help shape both the physical and informational dimensions of the battlespace. PSYOP provide a commander the means to employ a nonlethal capability across the range of military operations from peace through conflict to war and during postconflict operations. As information delivered for effect during peacetime and conflict, PSYOP inform and influence. When properly employed, PSYOP saves lives of friendly and adversary forces, whether military or civilian.

Department of the Army, FM 3-05.30, 'Psychological Operations', 1–2

how secure an individual feels in the environment around him. Obviously a combat zone is a particularly unsafe environment for all concerned, but if the weight of insecurity can be shifted onto the enemy, and he is made to feel helpless before opposing firepower and manoeuvre, then morale will wither.

Weaponry can have a particularly significant effect on the sense of safety. Investigation into the psychological impact of weaponry began in World War I, when whole new categories of ordnance entered the fray with a deplorable increase in levels of mortality. World War II continued the research. Work among

Psyops Warfare

Psychological warfare operations can be a valuable adjunct to conventional tools of force. Here, we see a US Army Humvee mounted with loudspeakers – these can be used for information broadcasts but also for inflicting sleep deprivation upon the enemy. Such aggressive transmissions were used by US Special Forces in Panama in the US invasion of 1989.

the Allies in the North African theatre threw up a fascinating spectrum of results, including which weapons men feared the most and how they adjusted to those weapons over a period of time.

The weapons judged 'most frightening' by 97 per cent of those evaluated were those that delivered shellfire (artillery and mortars) and bombing (aircraft). At the time of first combat experience of these weapons, air attack was the most alarming to 50 per cent of those involved; artillery was nominated by 20 per cent. Yet, only 11 days into battle those priorities had switched entirely as the soldiers became more familiar with the actual effects and capabilities of the weapons employed against them. (Artillery was both accurate and destructive, whereas dive-bombing was noisy and scary, but not as effective as artillery.) Further studies into the reasons why men feared weapons tended to show that accuracy, rapidity of fire and volume of noise were the primary sources of anxiety.

Devastating Attack

The types of weapons that attack the sense of safety have evolved since World War II. During the Coalition forces' operation to eject Iraqi troops from Kuwait in 1991, large numbers of Multiple Launch Rocket System (MLRS) artillery vehicles were used. A single rocket barrage from one of

Heavy Firepower

Heavy artillery and mortars are regularly judged to be the most alarming weapons to experience during combat. During World War II, around 50 per cent of soldiers classed artillery as the weapon that frightened them most. As artillery inflicted 70 per cent of casualties, their fears were justified.

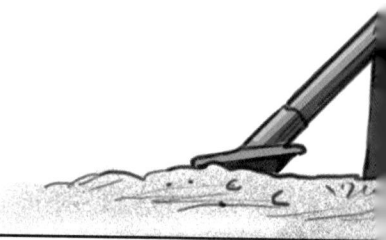

GMLRS Rocket Artillery

During the Gulf War of 1990–91, the devastating effects of strikes from the British and American Multiple Launch Rocket Systems (MLRS) caused mass psychological casualties among Iraqi forces. The airburst rockets led the Iraqis to nickname the weapons the 'black rain'.

Urban Devastation

Inflicting infrastructural damage can be an effective way of undermining the resolve of an opponent. As the Strategic Bombing Campaign of World War II demonstrated, however, such indiscriminate destruction rarely suffices to defeat an enemy, if his motivation to resist is strong enough.

these systems was virtually capable of destroying everything in a square kilometer of ground. The terrified Iraqi soldiers nicknamed the weapons 'Steel rain' on account of the thousands of lethal steel fragments showered down upon them by the airburst munitions. When ground troops then attacked through areas that had been saturated by the MLRS barrages, they discovered that the survivors were too mentally traumatized to put up an effective resistance. Most simply stuck their hands in the air and surrendered.

Note as well that safety is not just about the physical threats from weapons. There are many other types of safety instinct – financial, familial or safe accommodation, for example – and all can be disrupted by modern warfare. The most modern armies include soldiers trained in cyber warfare, attacking the enemy's computer and internet network or hacking into key IT systems. (It is a possibility, for example, that the Iranian nuclear energy/weapons programme has been seriously set back by the Stuxnet computer worm, the worm likely being of US military or Israeli origin.) If an enemy country's financial system can be compromised by military hackers, that in turn could disrupt public sector payments and thereby threaten the financial security of its soldiery.

The message, therefore, is that to compromise the enemy's sense of

Cyber Warfare

Modern armies are trained in cyber warfare, which enables soldiers to attack the enemy's internal structures from a safe distance. Future soldiers are going to need new levels of mental skill to handle cyber threats, with a premium placed on technological knowledge.

Reducing the Effects of 'Friction'

While we should attempt to minimize self-induced friction, the greater requirement is to fight effectively within the medium of friction. The means to overcome friction is the will; we prevail over friction through persistent strength of mind and spirit. While striving to overcome the effects of friction ourselves, we must attempt at the same time to raise our enemy's friction to a level that destroys his ability to fight.

We can readily identify countless examples of friction, but until we have experienced it ourselves, we cannot hope to appreciate it fully. Only through experience can we come to appreciate the force of will necessary to overcome friction and to develop a realistic appreciation for what is possible in war and what is not. While training should attempt to approximate the conditions of war, we must realize it can never fully duplicate the level of friction of real combat.

(MCDP 1, *Warfighting*, p.6).

ellbeing, as many angles as ossible must be attacked at the ame time. Furthermore, the attacks ust be delivered with speed and empo. These are not the same thing. peed is the rapidity with which an ttack is delivered. Tempo is the ace at which the operations are onducted over time. The objective r armies, both at the level of the dividual soldier and in terms of rger units, is to hit the opponent ster than they can respond, then maintain such a tempo of operations that the enemy is constantly on the back foot, reacting to events rather than seizing the initiative. In this way the enemy will not only be tactically outmanoeuvred, he will also likely acquire a forbidding sense of inferiority against the attackers, further weakening his sense of safety.

Higher Needs

The higher needs of the enemy occupy several strata of Maslow's

Moving Quickly

The speed with which this enemy stronghold is attacked means that there is less time for anyone to escape and fight back. Here, a squad uses a combination of grenades, small-arms fire and movement to overwhelm the trench complex.

hierarchy of needs, and they revolve around the more elevated functions of human consciousness. Typical elements of these levels include friendship, family, self-esteem, confidence, respect (both given and received), morality, creativity and religious beliefs. These might seem at a tangent to battlefield concerns, but actually they can be among the most powerful means of manipulating an enemy. Once again, Gray imparts some wisdom on this topic:

> *Although material factors are more easily quantified, the moral and mental forces exert a greater influence on the nature and outcome of war. This is not to lessen the importance of physical forces, for the physical forces in war can have a significant impact on the others. For example, the greatest effect of fires is generally not the amount of physical destruction they cause, but the effect of that physical destruction on the enemy's moral strength.*
> – MCDP 1, *Warfighting*, p.16

Attacking the enemy's higher levels of consciousness generally means an assault on things that are most important personally to each individual soldier, such as their family and sense of self-respect. During World War II, one factor that had a huge impact on the morale of German frontline soldiers was the Allied strategic bombing

Collateral damage

campaign against their homeland, which killed, wounded or rendered homeless literally millions of civilians. The soldiers' sense that they could do little to protect their loved ones, even

Soldiers in both Afghanistan and Iraq have had to adjust to the complexities of using heavy firepower in civilian areas. They must balance the severity of the threat with the likelihood of 'collateral damage' to civilians; the latter can be a key motivation for new generations of insurgent recruits. Here, Afghan civilians inspect the damage left by a US air strike.

as they fought for their own lives, had a crushing impact on their state of mind.

Acknowledging this fact does mean advocating a policy of targeting civilians, although the very fact that bombing campaigns are directed against infrastructure does contain this implication. In fact, hitting targets such as gas and water supplies, power stations, roads and electricity

Winning Hearts and Minds

Today's soldiers are trained in humanitarian skills, social care and even as de facto political ambassadors. The most important skill for soldiers on peacekeeping is that they are socially flexible and able to identify with people from any cultural or religious background.

pylons can have a profound effect on the mental wellbeing of an opponent. Take out electricity and telephone lines, for instance, and the enemy's sense of isolation from others increases as lines of communication are shut down. More brutally, snipers can undermine the confidence of an enemy military unit by systematically killing its officers and NCOs. Good leaders are at the core of a unit's morale, and once they are taken out of the equation, other, often less capable, men are overpromoted and by their subsequent actions and uncertainty have an impact on the morale of the force.

'Hearts and Minds'

Also intrinsic to defeating an opponent is what we now call 'hearts and minds'

Local Liaison

Increasing the enemy's feelings of isolation and panic, when combined with forging positive relations with local communities, can make the crucial difference in an insurgency conflict. The critical goal for peacekeepers is building trust within the foreign community, thereby depriving the insurgents of indigenous support.

Critical Vulnerability

We want to attack the source of enemy strength, but we do not want to attack directly into that strength. We obviously stand a better chance of success by concentrating our strength against some relative enemy weakness. So we also ask ourselves: Where is the enemy vulnerable? In battlefield terms, this means that we should generally avoid his front, where his attention is focused and he is strongest, and seek out his flanks and rear, where he does not expect us and where we can also cause the greatest psychological damage. We should also strike at a moment in time when he is vulnerable.

Of all the vulnerabilities we might choose to exploit, some are more critical to the enemy than others. Some may contribute significantly to the enemy's downfall while others may lead only to minimal gains. Therefore, we should focus our efforts against a critical vulnerability, a vulnerability that, if exploited, will do the most significant damage to the enemy's ability to resist us.

(MCDP 1, *Warfighting*, p.46).

operations. A hearts and minds campaign involves the soldiers – typically based in a foreign country – fostering good relations with the local population, with the long-term goal of turning the civilians against insurgents or even their own army. The British applied hearts and minds techniques to good effect in the Malayan Emergency (1948–60), isolating communist guerrillas from the rest of society and thereby starving the enemy of moral and material support during the conflict. In Vietnam, the US 5th Special Forces Group created numerous Civilian Irregular Defense Groups (CIDGs) composed of Vietnamese soldiers who were persuaded to fight for the South Vietnamese cause against the Viet Cong (VC) and North Vietnamese Army (NVA).

More recently, Coalition troops in Afghanistan have spent a great deal of time and money working on infrastructural projects to benefit the local populations, hoping to build table communities that turn off support for the Taliban.

Hearts and minds campaigns require patience, maturity and skill to implement, and can have slow and uncertain results. Soldiers must be educated that the values and ideas of their home country are not universal, and that they need to think from inside the host culture to see what their priorities are.

A successful hearts and minds campaign, however, can cut to the heart of an enemy's higher values and needs. Many young men join insurgent groups to gain the respect of others, for example, yet if the wider population eventually withdraws that respect, the motivation for the young man to keep fighting weakens. The message is that defeating an opponent requires an army to fight on every level of psychological need. Conversely, an invading army alienates itself from the population at its peril.

Killing an Enemy

The most profound act of controlling an enemy is, of course, to kill him or her. The effect of killing on the person doing it is not something that can be boiled down to easy principles. Many soldiers, at least during the actual act of combat, appear to be intoxicated not purely by the act of killing but by their ability to deliver extreme violence, making them feel alive and powerful in one heady package. A former soldier who fought in World War I, quoted by Joanna Bourke in the insightful book *An Intimate History of Killing*, spoke of this effect:

> *I had thought of myself more or less immune from this intoxication until, as a trench mortar officer, I was given command over what is probably the most murderous instrument in modern warfare... One day ... I secured a direct hit on an enemy encampment, saw bodies or parts of bodies go up into the air and heard the desperate yelling of the wounded or the runaways. I had to confess to myself that it was one of the happiest moments of my life.*

As Bourke's book reveals with great honesty, soldiers throughout history have often flushed with exhilaration at the act of killing, feeling, at least for a moment, as if they are gods. Of course, this is only one kind of reaction. Others are aware only of how little they feel after killing someone, regarding the act as no more or less significant than killing an insect. Others are shaken to the core by the enormity of what they have done, and left permanently traumatized. The response, it seems, is all down to the individual, although it can be guided to a significant degree by training and ideology.

Killer Instinct

Promoting and honing a killer instinct, while keeping this instinct under control for use at the appropriate time, is a challenge for the military. Soldiers must keep a clear distinction between combatants and civilians, even though actual combat experience frequently blurs this line.

On some level, killing the enemy has to be embraced if a soldier is to perform the job for which he was trained. Moreover, in many ways the possibility of combat is the reason why a soldier joined the armed services in the first place. To deny this fact is to deny the nature of soldiering. What commanders have to do, however, is control the process of killing so that it is kept within definable limits. If such control isn't in place, there is a greater possibility of units being involved in what we classify as atrocities.

Extreme Killing

All armies through history, to a greater or lesser degree, have committed actions that we today classify as atrocities. At one end of the spectrum are the Nazi police and SS death squads, who literally murdered millions in cold blood in Eastern Europe during 1941–42 as part of a deliberate and authorized policy. More commonly, there are those actions that occur on a smaller scale in remote corners of the battlefield or theatre, when soldiers' appetites for revenge or racial hatred tip over into excesses of killing.

One of the facts about the Vietnam War that so shocked the American public was the emerging evidence that US soldiers had on many occasions participated in bloodletting, rape and torture without military purpose, and against civilians as much as combatants. The dreadful pinnacle of

Soldier Shows Character and Discipline

On the morning of 28 February 1991, about a half-hour prior to the cease-fire, a T-55 tank pulled up in front of a US Bradley-equipped unit, which immediately prepared to engage with TOW missiles. A vehicle section consisting of the platoon sergeant and his wingman tracked the Iraqi tank, ready to unleash two deadly shots. Suddenly, the wingman saw the T-55 tank stop and a head popped up from the commander's cupola. The wingman immediately radioed to his platoon sergeant to hold his fire, believing that the Iraqi was about to dismount the vehicle, possibly to surrender.

The Iraqi tank crew jumped off their vehicle and ran behind a sand dune. Sensing something was not right, the platoon sergeant immediately instructed his wingman to investigate the area around a nearby dune, while he provided cover with his weapons. To everyone's surprise, the wingman and his crew soon discovered 150 enemy combatants ready to surrender. To deal with this large number of prisoners, the American unit lined them up and ran them through a gauntlet to disarm them and check them for items of intelligence value. Then the unit called for prisoner of war handlers to pick them up. Before moving on, the platoon sergeant had to destroy the T-55 tank. Before blowing it up, the NCO instructed it moved behind a sand berm to protect his people and the prisoners from the shrapnel of the tank's on-board munitions. When the tank suddenly exploded and the small arms cooked-off, sounding as if small arms were fired, the prisoners panicked, believing the soldiers would shoot them. Quickly, the soldiers communicated that this would not happen, one of them telling the Iraqis, 'Hey, we're from America, we don't shoot our prisoners!'

- US Army, 'Army Leadership: Confident, Competent, and Agile', FM 6-22 (October 2006) 4-1-4-2

the revelations related to events at the Vietnamese village of My Lai on 16 March 1968. On that day, anywhere between 347 and 504 Vietnamese civilians, mostly women, children and the elderly, were slaughtered by a company of soldiers from the Americal Division. The horror only came to the American public's attention months later, but it dealt a further body blow to

Inflicting Destruction

US soldiers destroy a building in which an insurgent unit is hiding. The key combat aims of a military unit are to obtain tactical dominance and fire superiority over the enemy. Accomplishing these can involve ignoring natural instincts for compassion, and a hardening of attitude towards human suffering.

the US Government's commitment to the Vietnam War.

The causes of atrocities are complex and vary according to each incident, although the following are frequently common factors:

- **Group morality** Groups are more likely to commit atrocities than individuals, when individual morality is suspended for the morality of the group.
- **Weak leadership** If officers appear complicit or just uncaring about violent behaviour towards civilians or prisoners, some soldiers can interpret those

Controlling Prisoners

Even as prisoners, the enemy needs to be handled with discipline. Here, a British unit is maintaining the strict separation of prisoners – so they cannot exchange information or prepare mutual cover stories. The captors must also ensure that they do not engage in such friendly terms with prisoners that security procedures are relaxed.

attitudes as a green light for their actions.

- **Revenge** Units involved in atrocities have often suffered recent or heavy casualties, and they therefore want to return pain to the enemy.
- **Frustration** A lack on contact

with the enemy, who has nevertheless inflicted casualties remotely through IEDs or other devices, can produce an uncontrollable anger once a unit comes into contact with prisoners or what are deemed sympathetic civilians.

- **Fatigue** Sheer exhaustion and sleep deprivation make people more likely to behave in ways that aren't consistent with their typical personality.
- **Racism** In armies with a particularly nationalistic or racial ideology, foreign people can be dehumanized so that killing them is somehow seen as inconsequential or justified.
- **PTSD** Soldiers suffering from the effects of post-traumatic stress disorder are more prone to breakdowns in self-control.

This list is partial, and can be affected by many different political, social and psychological factors. The problem for commanders is that once soldiers begin killing on a regular basis, it is often hard to turn the instinct off like a tap when needed. There are, however, measures that can be put in place to mitigate all these factors.

A critical factor in controlling the killing instinct is the example set by officers. Officers need to demonstrate the values of the army in their best expression, and show both the warrior spirit and a humane attitude towards civilians and prisoners. Even if the other side do not always observe human rights, the officer should make it clear that his unit stands for higher values. The actual nature of these values are discussed in detail in Chapter 4, but the unit commander should guide his soldiers to act as model representatives of their country.

Heat of the Moment

One of the moments when atrocities are most likely to be committed is just after combat, when adrenalin is still running strong and weapons are still hot from battle. In this tense atmosphere, soldiers are apt to turn to firepower as a first resort. Commands to cease fire, therefore, need to be circulated emphatically down through the unit, with specific instructions about the treatment of prisoners. Most important is that only individuals trained in interrogation techniques should be placed in charge of prisoners, and the prisoners should be sent quickly back behind the lines where they will be secure.

For those units who have suffered recent or heavy casualties, combat leaders need to keep a close eye out for the signs of combat stress reaction (CSR) setting in (see Chapter 7). Aggressive behaviour, disciplinary problems, substance abuse and

The Heat of Combat

A French soldier engages a target from his bunker. Just as important as training men to pull the trigger is training them to cease fire as soon as they are ordered to do so. It is in tense, chaotic battle situations that most of the atrocities of war take place. Mental endurance and self-control are never as important as when the fighting stops.

other similar infractions need to be dealt with quickly and decisively, often by removing the affected individuals temporarily from their unit. Appropriate periods of rest and recuperation, and counselling as required, will restore some perspective to events and prevent anxieties bubbling over into violence.

One final and important point in controlling soldier violence is

education. Units should be given some insight and involvement in local communities, with native customs explained to break down the sense of being in an alien culture. Time spent talking with locals is also time well spent, as it reveals that despite the cultural differences, people still share much in common with one another.

Defeating an opponent in battle, as we have seen in this chapter, involves far more than simply inflicting death and destruction on the enemy. If soldiers apply pressure to every aspect of an enemy's mental make-up, from his need to sleep, wash and eat, to his belief in self-expression and his ability to protect family at home, the chances of victory are significant. All the soldier needs to understand is that the enemy is also attempting to do the same in return.

Deployment to severe environments is part and parcel of being a modern soldier. Since 2003, many Western militaries have had to adjust to life in Iraq under scorching desert conditions. Those sent to Afghanistan have experienced an even greater spectrum of climate and terrain, from arctic-like blizzards in the mountainous regions to blisteringly hot, dusty valleys in the summer. Little wonder, therefore, that survival training forms a central component of Special Forces instruction.

The SAS carries out rigorous physical and mental training procedures as part of their selection process, so tough that only about 10 out of 125 applicants pass. The environments include the Brecon Beacons in Wales, where fitness and navigation are tested, followed by Belize, Central America, for jungle training, which develops tropical survival skills. The final phase for the small quota that make it through both ordeals is escape and evasion, during which candidates have three days to cross

....

However physically and mentally prepared for battle you may be, living and working in foreign environments can be the ultimate test of mental endurance, the nature of the terrain presenting unique psychological challenges.

6

Never will you be tested as thoroughly as when you are up against nature. Approaching the environment with the right mindset can be the difference between success and failure.

Environmental and Physical Challenges

Amphibious Team

Aquatic operations need men who are utterly at home in water. Not every soldier has such qualities. Battling against rough coastal currents, as seen in this US Navy SEAL team, is intensely frustrating, and requires men with physical stamina as well as knowledge of the sea.

terrain via a series of waypoints without being captured.

Whether captured or not, at the end each candidate must endure tactical questioning and interrogation while not giving anything away (name, rank, serial number and date of birth is the limit to the response). The whole process lasts approximately six months and pressure-tests physical strength, self-motivation and mental toughness. As we shall see in this chapter, survival is as much about psychological resilience as practical wilderness skills.

Environmental Factors

The sometimes-overwhelming power of nature should never be underestimated. Cold, heat, altitude and wet weather can have a profoundly negative and lasting effect on a soldier's mood and mental endurance. Freak conditions can threaten an entire operation and cost lives, such as occurred within the well-documented Bravo Two Zero SAS squadron, operating in Iraq in 1991. (Two soldiers died of hypothermia when the region was swept with snowstorms.) Unfortunately, tough conditions and war zones often go hand in hand, so the more you know about your environment, the more you can mentally and physically prepare yourself. Knowledge, therefore, is the first line of survival.

Desert Terrain

Deserts present as much of a mental challenge as a physical one. Many deserts can reach up to 55°C (131°F) routinely during the day, dropping rapidly to near freezing over night. (The same low humidity and lack of cloud cover that make the desert so hot also allows the desert to lose heat quickly.) There are desert regions on over one-third of the Earth's land surface, with more than 50 major deserts across the world, the largest of which is the Sahara in northern Africa.

Surviving, let alone working, in such conditions can test your endurance levels. A key point – applicable to all extreme terrains – is never to overestimate your physical strength to endure harsh climatic conditions. No matter how tough you are, there is a scientific reality to the effects of prolonged exposure to direct sunlight and equatorial heat. Treat the desert with respect at all times, and put in place procedures to minimize the danger from the environment. For example, aim to carry out the most physically demanding work during the early morning, evening and night when it is cooler, and try to stay under cover during the hottest part of the day (usually 10am to 3pm). Dress as comfortable and cool as you can by wearing light, loose clothing that covers as much of your body as possible.

The World's Deserts

Great Basin

Peruvian

Atacama

Patagonian

Approximately one-third of the world's land surface is taken up by desert regions. These include some of the most deadly terrains anywhere on Earth, which present intense challenges to military forces.

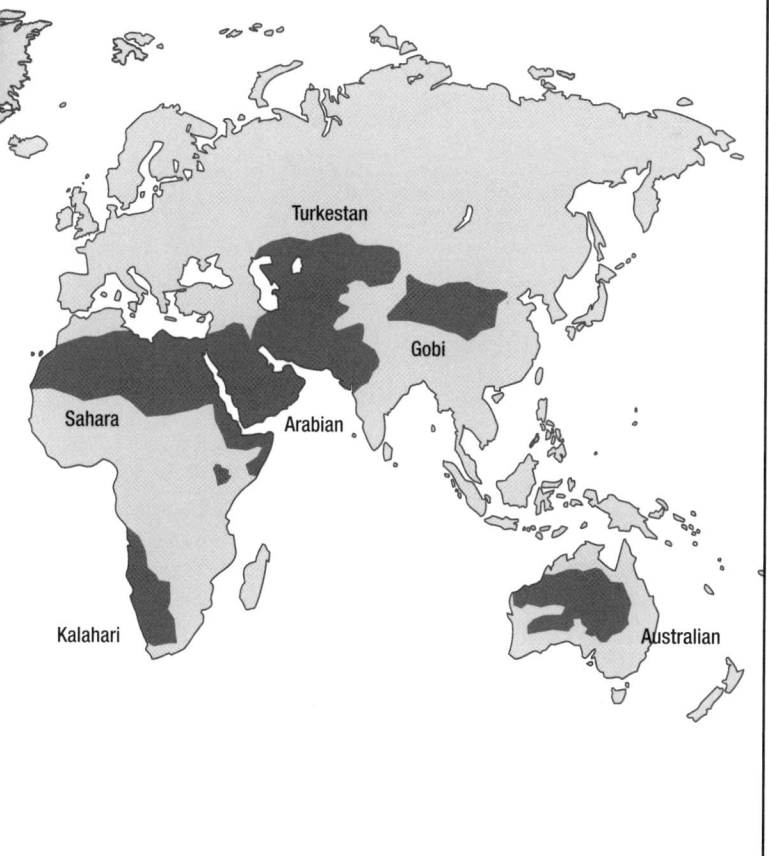

Desert Combat Wear

The approriate uniform can mean the difference between comfort and misery in the desert. You must remain shielded from the sun at all times, hence the right headgear is paramount.

It is also essential that you keep your head covered at all times. Direct sunlight on the scalp, as well as running the risk of heat stroke, can lead to severe headaches and mental confusion. Similarly, avoid baring skin to the sun – especially if you aren't used to strong sunlight – even when sunscreen is used. You might feel that you can handle a bit of heat, but the pain of sunburn will act as

a distraction when webbing straps are biting down hard on it.

Mental Demands in Desert Operations

The peculiar nature of operations in desert terrain is as much about handling mental disorientation as it is about practical challenges. This being said, the US Army Field Manual FM 90-3 *Desert Operations* provides

Tip: Royal Geographical Society Risk Assessment

Here is an assessment guide to potential risks based on one provided by the Royal Geographical Society (RGS) Expedition Handbook. The RGS recommend that you go through all the 'what if' scenarios so that you are prepared and know what to do if something goes wrong; and have the necessary equipment and supplies. What follows is a list of the dangers and situations to evaluate in any expedition or adventure.

The Team
• Health and fitness (including previous medical conditions) – increased risk of existing health problems on expedition, leading to serious illness / death
• Attitude and behaviour – increased risk of ignoring control measures, resulting in illness / injury
• Experience and training – reduces risk

Personal equipment
• Serious injury / illness resulting from inadequate equipment / equipment failure

The Environment
• Mountains / sea / desert / jungle
• Altitude sickness / drowning / heat problems
• Climate and weather conditions
• Heat- and cold-related injury / death

Health
• Endemic diseas
• Polluted water
• Contaminated food
• Hygiene / living conditions

Edible Desert Plants

Soldiers in desert regions needs to acquire as much knowledge as possible about their environment. For example, the plants below are edible, but sit amongst numerous poisonous varieties.

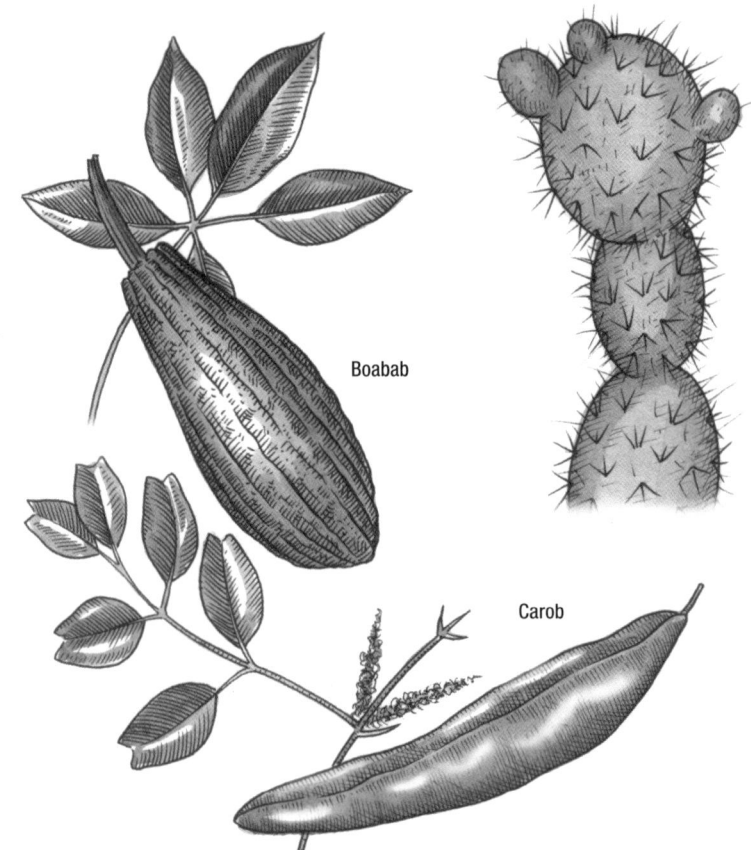

Prickly pear

Boabab

Carob

some initial reassurance about such environments:

There is no reason to fear the desert environment, and it should not adversely affect the morale of a soldier/marine who is prepared for it. Lack of natural concealment has been known to induce temporary agoraphobia (fear of open spaces) in some troops new to desert conditions, but this fear normally disappears with acclimatization.

Remember that there is nothing unique about either living or fighting in deserts; native tribesmen have lived in the Sahara for thousands of years. The British maintained a field army and won a campaign in the Western Desert in World War II at the far end of a 12,000-mile sea line of communication with equipment considerably inferior to that in service now. The desert is neutral, and affects both sides equally; the side whose personnel are best prepared for desert operations has a distinct advantage. – FM 90-3, 1-17

In balance to such sound advice, deserts nevertheless remain harsh environments in which to serve, and prolonged exposure to the sapping heat, clouds of flies and stark landscape can have a significant effect on morale over time. Troops serving in North Africa during World War II often reported a heavy sense of desolation and alienation while operating in the most barren regions. This is partly on account of the sheer hostility of the terrain and the lack of anything that reminds of home. There are also some unpalatable facts about desert combat. Skin diseases and gastric complaints are common, eroding a soldier's energy and morale. Food tends to become contaminated with sand and dust, resulting in a reduction in the pleasure of eating. The dead, if not buried quickly, soon decompose under the equatorial heat, adding a further touch of horror to the environment.

Acclimatization

Acclimatization is the key to mental adjustment to the desert, along with the recognition that the enemy is suffering under the same conditions as you are. Combat leaders should give clear explanations of why the soldiers are deployed to that theatre and what they hope to achieve there. Above all, leaders need to enforce rigorous standards of hygiene and physical discipline if they are to prevent the perennial banes of desert life – disease, sunburn, dehydration and heatstroke. The *Desert Operations* manual is once again clear on this point:

Commanders must pay special attention to the welfare of troops

operating in the desert, as troops are unable to find any 'comforts' except those provided by the command. Welfare is an essential factor in the maintenance of morale in a harsh environment, especially to the inexperienced. There is more to welfare than the provision of mail and clean clothing. Troops must be kept healthy and physically fit, they must have adequate, palatable, regular food and be allowed periods of rest and sleep. These things will not always be possible and discomfort is inevitable, but if troops know that their commanders are doing everything they can to make life tolerable, they will more readily accept the extremes brought on by the environment.
– FM 90-3, Desert Operations, 1-18

This passage contains a wealth of practical advice for a commander wanting to ensure the wellbeing of his troops in a desert theatre. The point about comforts is particularly critical. Given the stark nature of the terrain, and the fact that many desert deployments are a long way from the bright lights and interest of civilization, a desert base or outpost requires some innovation to have even the suggestion of homeliness. Much depends on the nature of the base. A major Main

Operating Base (MOB) – defined by the US military as 'an overseas, permanently manned, well protected base, used to support permanently deployed forces, and with robust sea and/or air access'– is likely have have all the amenities available to an affluent military nation. These include satellite TV, major catering facilities, recreational centres (such as gyms and bars), access to nearby cities, a hospital and effective communications with home. Moving nearer the frontline, however, and we enter the world of the Forward Operating Base (FOB). An FOB is a secure military base used to support nearby tactical operations. Given its operational purpose, life at an FOB tends to be far more spartan than that experienced at an MOB. The catering facilities might produce a fairly limited and monotonous range of food stuffs, and the only recreational facility could be a rudimentary gym or a basketball court scraped into the dust. Communications with home are typically strictly limited, often on the basis of brief weekly access to e-mail or an internet/satellite phone (mobile phones tend to be forbidden in operational areas), although the military mail system is usually faithfully maintained. For soldiers at the very hard edge of the frontline, inhabiting active Patrol Bases (PBs) or Checkpoints (CPs), the standards of living can descend into the positively medieval. In these circumstances the soldier might find himself spending days, even weeks, without bathing or showering, having to squat over rudimentary latrine pits dug into the earth, and with little to eat but MREs.

As is obvious from this description, there are distinct mental challenges for those facing life in an FOB, PB or CB, especially if these are located in featureless desert terrain, which adds blistering heat to the list of maladies. Measures to reduce some of the mental strain of this existence are as follows:

- Chances for the men to be both on their own and to relax together as a group.
- Encouraging humour – any absurd practices or pastimes that improve morale without reducing security are to be promoted.
- The environment should be improved as much as possible. For example, if a satellite phone is available, building a booth around it will allow the soldiers to talk with their families in relative privacy.
- If the soldiers occupy static positions, there should be regular periods of exercise – physical exertion aids both stress reduction and improves morale through good health.
- The positions need to provide as much protection from the

environment as possible, such as fly nets, overhead cover from the sun, properly constructed latrines and good supplies of fresh drinking water.
- Rehydration needs to take place on a regular basis, as poor hydration leads to adverse changes in mental state.
- The diet should be as varied as possible, although giving soldiers an erratic mix of home-cooked food and MREs can confuse the digestion as well as the emotions.

The procedural diligence extends to equipment as well, given the destructive effects of wind-blown dust and sand, as the *Desert Operations* manual makes clear:

> *Dust and sand adversely affect the performance of weapons. Weapons may jam or missiles lock on launching rails due to sand and dust accumulation. Sand- or dust-clogged barrels can lead to in-bore detonations. Daily supervised cleaning of weapons is essential. Particular attention should be given to magazines that are often clogged, interrupting the feeding of weapons. Cover missiles on launchers until they are required for use. To avoid jamming due to the accumulation of sand, the working parts of weapons must have the absolute minimum*

amount of lubrication. It may even be preferable to have them totally dry, as any damage caused during firing will be less than that produced by a sand/oil abrasive paste. Paintbrushes are among the most useful tools to bring to the desert, as they are extremely effective in cleaning weapons and optics.
– FM 90-3, 1-36

The manual goes on to describe the deleterious effects of dust and sand on everything from computer drives to optical sights. Obscuration resulting from heat haze or dust can also have a detrimental impact on the accuracy of fire control, particularly for artillery and tank crews. For example, an artillery observer calling in indirect fire needs to ensure that the first ranging shots land beyond the target to prevent short rounds throwing up dust and obscuring the target. Desert conditions therefore require great mental discipline on the part of all involved. Routines need to be put in place for cleaning and hygiene, and these need to be followed to the letter.

Staying Hydrated
The importance of staying hydrated was discussed in Chapter 3 in relation to fluid loss during exercise. Hydration is especially important if you are physically exerting yourself in hot climates, where you should drink

Withdrawal

Cold-weather conditions raise the danger of a soldier withdrawing into himself, mentally escaping the harsh conditions. While a short period of reverie is fine, NCOs and officers must motivate the men to face challenges realistically and directly, and keep their energies focused on purposeful activity.

Remaining Calm

Remaining calm, and keeping thought processes logical, are critical to surviving severe climates. Even under the severe stress of being trapped in an avalanche, this soldiers remains purposeful, using a swimming action to keep his head above the snow.

between 6 and 8 litres (12–16 pints) of water a day. Keep fluid intake as high as possible and spread your drinking at regular intervals, taking in little, but often. Also, keep a close eye on the water supply and stick to a strict ration as soon as low supplies become an issue. Dehydration can be deadly, so utilize whatever natural resources are available if bottled supplies become scarce.

Sub-zero Conditions

Sub-zero conditions present as many mental and physical challenges as desert conditions, albeit of a very different nature. The obvious priority is to stay warm and healthy, avoiding the dangers of hypothermia and frostbite. Normal body temperature is around 37°C (98.6°F). If core body temperature falls below 35°C (95°F), hypothermia can begin to set in. Signs of hypothermia are mental as well as physical and include shivering, lack of muscle coordination, lethargy and slow movements, confusion, pale skin or even blue-tinged extremities as blood vessels contract to retain heat.

The effects of sub-zero conditions on an unprepared army can be little short of catastrophic. Hannibal's army lost nearly half its troops in 218 BCE when crossing the Pyrenean Alps. Napoleon's army lost tens of thousands of men to hypothermia during its retreat from Moscow in the winter of 1812, and environment-

Winter Combat

A camouflaged sniper takes aim from a snowy foxhole. Cold-weather climates add numerous extra mental and physical burdens to operations. For example, this soldier needs to exercise digilent weapon-cleaning procedures to prevent his rifle freezing solid.

Layering

The layering principle offers you the best way of controlling and preserving body heat.

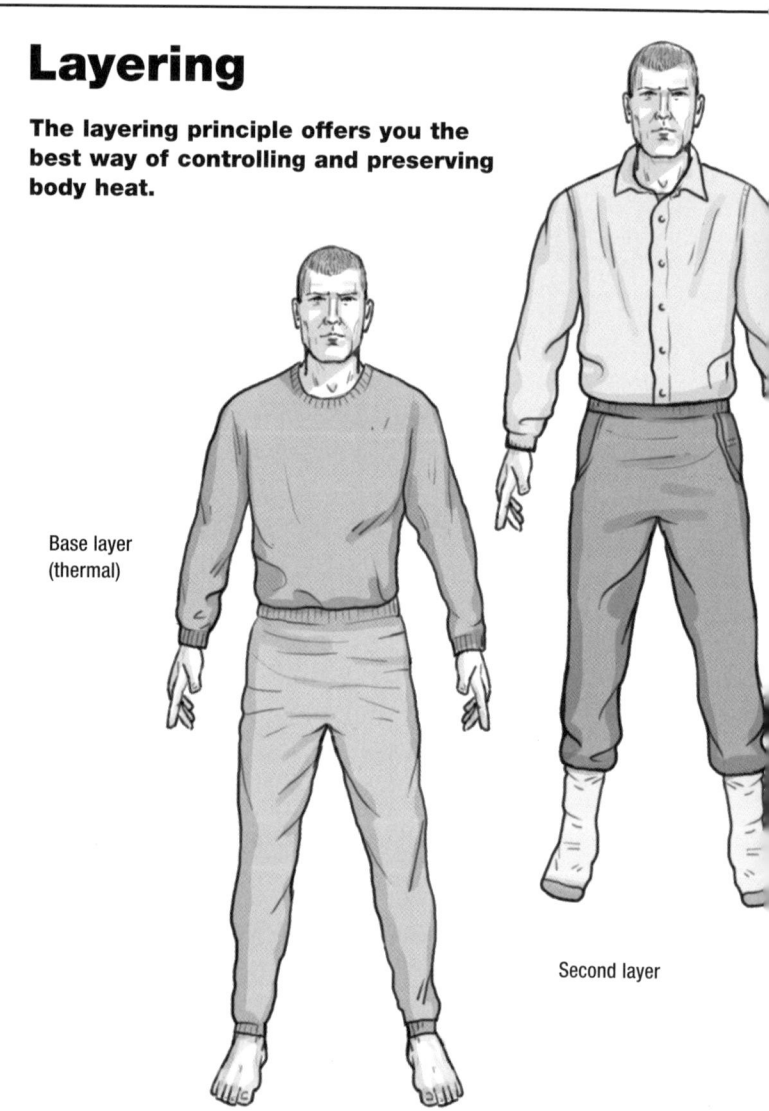

Base layer
(thermal)

Second layer

The British Army CS95 uniform, for example, consists of seven different items, ranging from a thermal-vest base layer to an outer Gore-Tex jacket.

Weatherproof layer

Fleece layer

Arctic Clothing

Survival in arctic climates depends on a disciplined approach to every aspect of clothing. Each soldier must take special care with his or her clothing, wearing appropriate items and keeping everything in good repair. Your clothing needs to be waterproof, windproof and have a high level of heat retention. Outer layers for both jacket and trousers should be both water- and windproof. The US armed forces are issued with Extended Cold Weather Clothing System (ECWCS), which is suitable for temperatures ranging from around 4 to -51°C (40 to -60°F). The key to heat retention in the ECWCS, just as in civilian cold weather clothing, is layering. A lightweight base layer, mid-weight shirt and trousers, fleece jackets and cold/wet weather-proof top layers of parka and trousers are recommended. Avoid heavy fabrics such as denim or cotton, which take a long time to dry if they get wet.

related losses among German forces in the winter of 1941–42 in Russia and Ukraine for a time outstripped combat casualties.

Mental Withdrawal

Many of the problems that surrounded these campaigns were due to lack of forethought or preparation. (During Germany's Operation *Barbarossa* against the Soviet Union in 1941, for example, Hitler expected the campaign to be essentially complete before the winter. As it was, German troops went into one of the cruellest winters in decades in mainly summer uniforms.) Today, military personnel are generally much better prepared, with fast and efficient methods of preventing and treating hypothermia. Yet avoiding hypothermia is naturally your first aim. Stay warm and dry, replace wet clothing regularly and seek shelter from severe winds – wind chill accelerates the body's loss of heat.

A fascinating insight into the nature of sub-zero operations comes from the 1990 report for the Naval Health Research Center by R.R. Vickers, Jr, D.W. Kolar and D.L. Kelleher, *Coping Strategies and Mood During Cold Weather Training*. A psychological evaluation was conducted between two military training groups, one operating in sub-zero winter conditions and the other in summer mountain environments. The report came to some decisive conclusions about the nature of cold-weather training:

(a) *Anger, Fear/Anxiety, and Depression were higher during cold weather training, and Happiness and Activity were lower during this training. The exception to the general trend was that fatigue was comparable in both training groups.*

(b) *Cold weather trainees reported more escapist thinking about better times and places, and there was a trend toward less frequent problem solving and planning in the cold.*

(c) *Positive moods were higher among men who employed problem solving and related coping strategies; negative moods were higher among men who employed escapist thinking and related coping strategies.*
- Ross Vickers et al., *Coping Strategies and Mood During Cold Weather Training*, 1990

Arctic Acclimatization

For troops who have completed their unit and combined training, considerable training in snow and cold is necessary before a unit is proficient under such conditions; during this training, cross country movements without shelter in buildings during halts must be practiced. On the march, individuals should be equipped to be self-sustaining, carrying their own food and shelter.

While friendly personnel are weakened in strength and morale by cold, fatigue and hunger, this is equally true of the enemy. Whenever possible, the enemy should be denied the use of towns or buildings. Patrols, aircraft and harassing fire should be used against him in bivouacs, and constant raids should prey on his supply system. Every possible means should be employed to deprive him of food, rest and shelter. He will make corresponding efforts against our troops, and means of repulsing these efforts must be employed.

- FM 70-15, 'Operations in Snow and Extreme Cold' (1944) p.84

Arctic Survival

This soldier is able to stay reasonably warm and protected from harm in this snow cave. Note the different sections for sleeping and sitting, which raise him off the ground, plus the layers of fabric between his body and the snow. Knowing how to take control of your environment can be a vital tool to help you stay mentally strong.

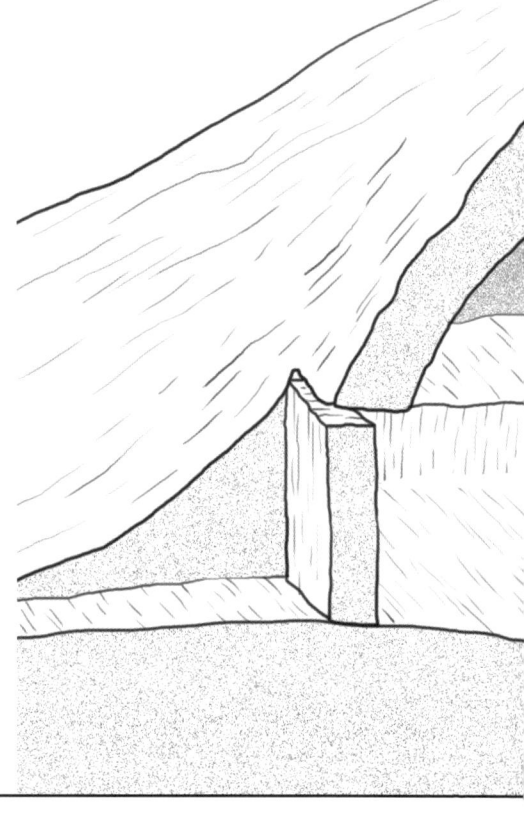

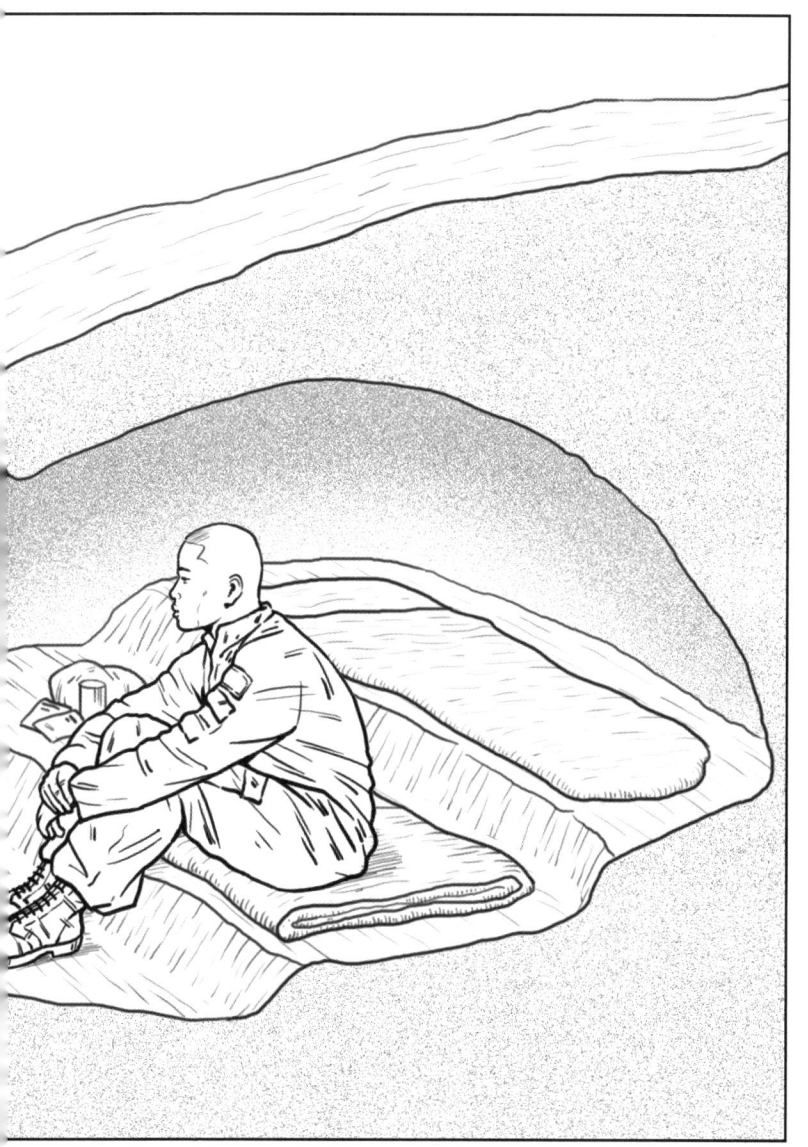

This passage makes it clear that cold weather is hard on the emotions. The very hostility of the environment causes human beings to withdraw inside themselves, indulging in 'escapist thinking' and slipping into anger and depression. The reasons for this are not hard to spot amongst any soldier who has conducted arctic operations. The time and effort taken to perform tasks multiplies tremendously in freezing, icy conditions. Gloves have to be worn at all times, reducing manual dexterity. Bulky clothing affects freedom of movement. Deep snow makes even the very act of walking difficult. Weapons and equipment can freeze up, requiring time-consuming processes to make them operable.

Raising Morale

The report also evaluated different forms of coping mechanism amongst the participants. Those who coped best used an array of strategies. These included humour, making a positive assessment of the challenges, talking with friends about problems, being proactive in problem solving, accepting that the situation is temporary and simple emotional control.

One elemental way of raising morale, if combat conditions allow, is to light a blazing campfire in the evening. Not only does this provide a useful means of cooking, it also warms the body as much as the spirits. Open fires are also known for their calming effect, creating a space for reflection and adjustment. One useful tip is to build a rock or log wall near the fire; if the soldiers stand between the fire and the wall, the wall will reflect heat onto their backs, creating a cocoon of warmth. Warming food and drink also play an important role in mental composure. Try to consume all meals hot and at regular intervals – the expectation of hot food at predictable times of day will make the intervening periods more bearable.

Adequate shelter is obviously a priority in arctic conditions for sheer survival as much as morale. If the shelter is something as basic as a snow cave (a habitable space dug into the side of a deep snow drift) then use plentiful fir branches to line the walls and floors, making the surroundings more welcoming. Basic lighting, even in the form of a few candles, will also raise the mood of even the harshest shelter, but ensure that all shelters have adequate ventilation to avoid the risk of suffocation.

Mountainous Terrain

The weather in mountain ranges can be extreme and changeable, hence only the most specialized mountain troops tend to be deployed there. A direct mental challenge of mountain environments is that of precipitous drops. Those who suffer from acrophobia (fear of heights) are

Cold Weather Kit

The right clothing is not just a matter of keeping warm and physically safe. It also gives the wearer a sense of confidence that he can face his environment and triumph over it. Ensure that all equipment is well maintained, kept free of dirt and in a good state of repair. Poor clothing management usually indicates a collapse in discipline.

Coping in a Mountain Environment

Acclimatizing to altitude is the most critical element of mountain survival. The physical effects of altitude sickness can include nausea, headaches and dizziness, and it can even be fatal if the casualty isn't taken to lower altitudes rapidly. Altitude also affects energy levels – this ski trooper will experience increased respiration and heart rate while operating in mountain environments, compared to sea-level terrains.

unlikely to have made it through basic training for a mountain unit. Rappelling towers alone can range from 9m to over 15m (34–50ft), which may not sound too high in theory, but it can seem very different when you are standing on top of one. A drop of several hundred metres from a narrow mountain ledge therefore tests even the strongest nerves.

Training

Training for mountain warfare skills is generally a gradual progression, working from simple climbing towers up to major mountain expeditions. Fear of falling, however, can take hold of even experienced climbers. The advice 'don't look down' is as practical as it is familiar; when looking down a drop, the brain can struggle to rationalize the perspective between its current position and the mountain floor, resulting in a sensation of vertigo.

Breathe calmly and deeply until the panic subsides. Then focus all your concentration on the climbing skills you have learnt, knowing that they will keep you safe if you stick to their rules. Officers should also take a lead, providing technical and morale guidance when conditions become dangerous.

The greatest threat to life on a high-altitude mountain, however, comes not from falls, or even landslide or avalanche, but rather altitude itself. Altitude or mountain

Mountain Regions of the World

Covering vast terrains in most of the world's continents, mountainous regions are particularly harsh on body and mind. They produce similar psychological effects to those experienced generally in cold-weather climates – depression, a sense of isolation and the threat of mentally withdrawing from reality.

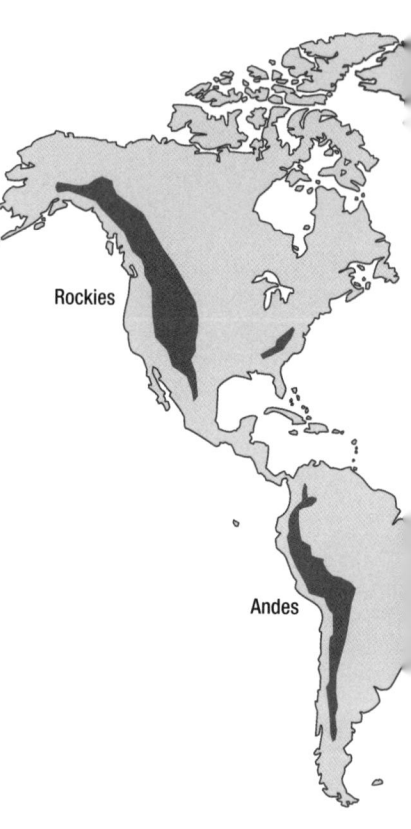

Rockies

Andes

sickness is caused by ascending into high altitudes too quickly, without giving the body time to adjust and acclimatize. Higher altitudes have lower levels of oxygen, so the body has to work much harder to supply sufficient oxygen to the brain, blood and muscles.

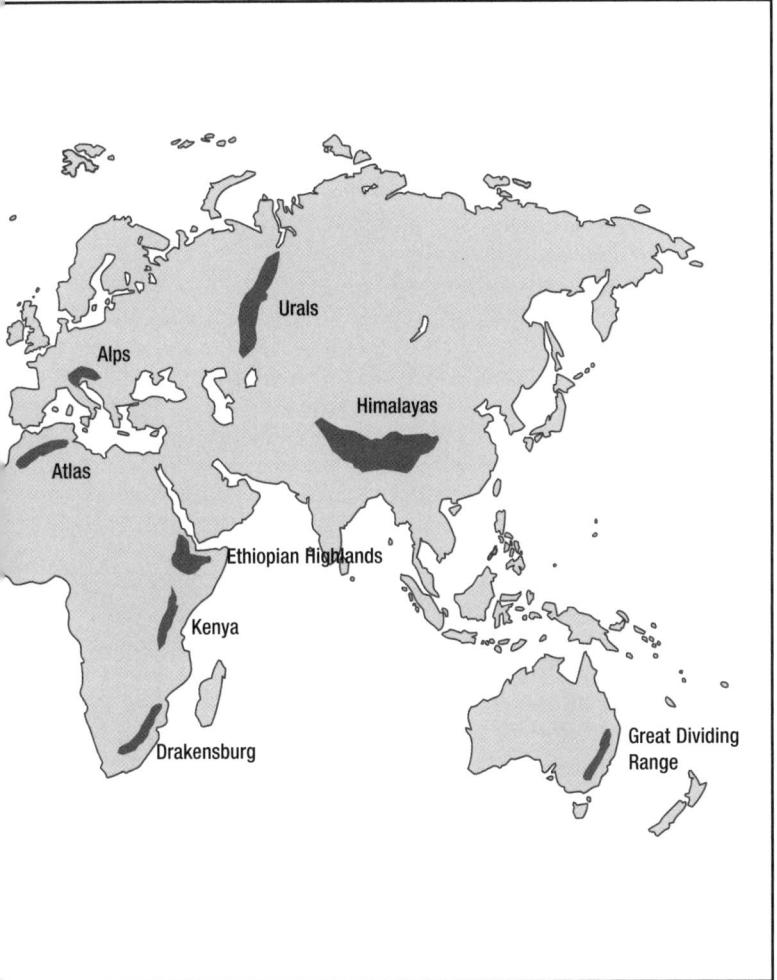

Altitude sickness generally kicks in at 2400m (8000ft) above sea level, especially if you are ascending at a rate of more than 300m (1000ft) a day. To put this into context, Mount Everest in the Himalayas is 8848m (29,029ft) high, meaning it should take you at least 30 days to ascend

Mountain Nutrition

1-31. Poor nutrition contributes to illness or injury, decreased performance, poor morale and susceptibility to cold injuries, and can severely affect military operations. Influences at high altitudes that can affect nutrition include a dulled taste sensation (making food undesirable), nausea and lack of energy or motivation to prepare or eat meals.

1-32. Caloric requirements increase in the mountains due to both the altitude and the cold. A diet high in fat and carbohydrates is important in helping the body fight the effects of these conditions. Fats provide long-term, slow caloric release, but are often unpalatable to soldiers operating at higher altitudes. Snacking on high-carbohydrate foods is often the best way to maintain the calories necessary to function.

1-33. Products that can seriously impact soldier performance in mountain operations include:

- **Tobacco** Smoking interferes with oxygen delivery by reducing the blood's oxygen-carrying capacity. Tobacco smoke in close, confined spaces increases the amounts of carbon monoxide. The irritant effect of tobacco smoke may produce a narrowing of airways, interfering with optimal air movement. Smoking can effectively raise the 'physiological altitude' as much as several hundred meters.
- **Alcohol** Drinking alcohol impairs judgement and perception, depresses respiration, causes dehydration and increases susceptibility to cold injury.
- **Caffeine** May improve physical and mental performance but caffeine also causes increased urination (leading to dehydration) and, therefore, should be consumed in moderation.

– *Mountain Operations* (2000)

safely without altitude sickness. This does not take into account any other factors such as the extreme cold weather conditions, rest days and level of physical endurance.

Altitude sickness can initially present itself through a mix of physical and mental symptoms, including:

- shortness of breath
- fatigue
- headaches
- dizziness
- nausea
- decreased appetite

If left to develop, altitude sickness can develop into high-altitude pulmonary edema (HAPE), in which breathing problems lead to wet coughs, gurgling respiration and even pulmonary failure. HAPE can occur after as little as one day at high altitude. High-altitude cerebral

Free Climbing

An excellent test of both mental and physical endurance, free climbing is made easier by mentally plotting your route before you begin to climb. This way, you may spot holds and cracks that would be harder to see when you have begun the climb.

edema (HACE) – a swelling of the brain tissue – can also be fatal if left untreated. Symptoms include extreme fatigue and shortness of breath, impaired coordination and confusion followed by eventual coma and death.

Acclimatization is your most important defence against altitude sickness. This is the process of allowing your body to compensate for the lower oxygen levels in a gradual, progressive manner. A slow, graded ascent at 91m (300ft) a day is recommended to give the body time to get used to the lack of oxygen.

Watch out for bravado among members of a unit. Soldiers are a determined breed and can push themselves harder than their bodies actually allow. If a soldier exhibits signs of altitude sickness, as diagnosed by comrades or unit physicians, he should be sent immediately back down the mountain; even a few hundred feet of descent can make the difference between life and death.

Ignore any protestations about being fit to continue upwards – further increases in altitude will exacerbate the condition, and when the most serious signs become apparent, it can be too late to save a person's life.

The Tropics

Tropical environments, especially rainforests and jungles, present an especially threatening world for military operations. From a distance they can appear idyllic. Most areas have a wet or rainy season of up to a few months, promoting enormous growth of plant life. Vegetation is generally lush, green and diverse, as is animal life, and the surroundings can be of astonishing beauty. The downside is that disease proliferates easily, including killers such as malaria, cholera, typhus and dysentery. Biting, stinging and venomous creatures are found in huge numbers and varieties. The combination of high temperature and high humidity makes heat exhaustion a nagging threat, particularly to soldiers working their bodies hard on combat operations. Jungle terrain, rivers and swamps all have their own challenges and dangers. Sharp thorns can deliver deep penetrating wounds that can become quickly infected, and some plants, if carelessly eaten, can bring death from poisoning within 24 hours.

Jungle Apparel

In such an environment, the right clothing and equipment is essential, and once again combat leaders must be fastidious in implementing hygiene and sanitation regimes. Good boots are vital. They should be lightweight but strong and breathable. Metal plates or caps are often added to jungle boots to ensure nothing sharp penetrates the sole. Ensure that you

Climbing Techniques

- Climbing tests both mental agility and physical strength. As a climber, you should always keep in mind the following core principles:
- Read your route, looking for holds and taking your weight and reach into account.
- Keep your weight balanced over your feet, with your legs straight.
- Use your hands primarily for balance, generally keeping them in front of your shoulders.
- Aim to smoothly move only one part of your body at once (arm, leg or trunk).
- Test your hold before shifting full body weight.
- If your weight holds, shift your body weight to carry yourself forwards.
- Keep three points of contact with the surface at all times.
- Keep most of your weight on your feet, using your hands to keep you close to the rock face.
- Look for rest spots and build them into your climb.
- Practice taking a fall safely.

have several changes of socks, and replace wet socks with dry ones as soon and as often as you can. The same goes for clothing. High humidity means that you will sweat a lot, especially when you are on manoeuvres. Never sleep in sweat-soaked or wet clothes as this can promote skin infections. Change into a spare set overnight; the others should have dried by the morning. Heads should be covered in direct

Problem Solving Tip: Six Thinking Hats

This decision-making tool was developed by the logic expert Edward de Bono. The tool aims to extend the possibilities of problem solving by looking at problems from different perspectives. In each case, you have to imagine that you put on a particular hat, and that each hat relates to a specific mode of thinking.

White hat
• With this hat on, you look coldly and analytically at the available data, or in a crisis you may want to summarize and take stock of your situation, your supplies and so on.

Red hat
• With this hat on, you look at your position from an intuitive and emotional perspective, taking into account your own and others' gut reactions.

Black hat
• Look at your current situation and available options from a pessimistic standpoint. Look at the worse-case scenarios and what might go wrong if you embark on a particular course of action. Thinking with this hat should help you to be realistic about problems. For example, you may plan a long walk to safety, but you admit with your black hat on that two members of your group are not fit enough

sunlight and a handkerchief or bandana is useful for wiping or soaking up sweat.

The high density of jungle canopies means that although you will be sheltered, there is equal opportunity for enemy troops to be well hidden. A careful eye and ear must be kept out for ambushes. Well-trained soldiers are practised in looking *through* rather than *at* vegetation, using the thousands of

to do the distance. How will you get round that problem? With the black hat on you may hope for the best, but prepare for the worst.

Yellow hat
• This is the sunny hat. With this hat on, you look at all the positive sides of your situation and courses of action. For example, you may be stranded but you have enough food and water to last you a few days. How will you take advantage of that situation? In a crisis, looking at the positive side will be a morale booster for yourself and for others

Green hat
• This is the creative hat that allows plenty of scope for free thought and ideas. Sometimes this kind of thinking throws up possibilities that can be turned into practical reality.

Blue hat
• This hat represents the chair of the meeting, who may want to analyze the practical responsibilities in an otherwise wild idea or ask for more creative thinking if the ideas are too hidebound, cautious or pessimistic. For example, there is a river between you and safety. Going the long way round will mean a lengthy detour and you may not have enough supplies, or team members may be unfit or injured.

Jungle Training

The jungle environment can be acutely claustropobhic, with low light levels and visibility reduced to a matter of metres by the vegetation. The sense of threat is heightened by the fact that the enemy could be in close proximity but hidden from view. In such environments, soldiers need strong nerves and good training to survive.

Jungle training exercises such as river walking require mental stamina, bravery and determination. It is vital that each soldier retains a sense of combat readiness and becomes as familiar as he can with the terrain.

minute gaps between leaves and foliage to form a composite window through the jungle. This technique also has the benefit of reducing 'jungle claustrophobia', a common complaint among soldiers who spend week after week in a green twilight with visibility limited to just a few metres.

Dense canopies can also make navigation very difficult as the deceiving similarity of the paths and vegetation can be disorientating. Take regular bearings as you travel and don't lose track of the rest of the team. Progress can be slow, but moving safely is much more important than speed in this environment. Avoid travelling at night if possible and similarly avoid wading through swamps or water where you can, as these tend to be traps for disease.

The jungle can never be tamed, but as with the other extreme environments listed above, knowledge of the terrain and practical, beneficial routines ensure that life in the jungle is possible, if not comfortable.

Water Systems

Approximately 70 per cent of the Earth's surface is covered in water. It is highly likely that you will encounter it at some stage in your military career, be it in sea, river or lake systems. While this is especially relevant for Marines and the Navy, any member of the elite forces must be confident in water and have an understanding of water safety. If you cannot swim, are a weak swimmer or have a fear of water, then your military career is likely to be cut short. Each soldier will need to complete basic water survival training so that he or she is no threat to themselves or their unit during operations either in or around water. Ideally, you should be able to:

- Maintain buoyancy in full gear.
- Swim 15 yards (45 ft) underwater.
- Swim the travel stroke, breaststroke and sidestroke.
- Assist other swimmers in the water.
- Use personal safety and water survival techniques.
  (See Department of the Army, TC 21-21, *Water Survival Training*)

Soldiers should also follow the SAFE principle in all their swimming technique:

Slow, easy movement. This is critical for energy conservation.
Apply natural buoyancy. Let the water support the body.
Full lung inflation. Keep the lungs inflated to help maintain buoyancy.
Extreme relaxation. This ensures more control and composure.

Life Raft

The standard military lifeboat kit includes survival tools for staying healthy, procuring food and returning to safety. Those aboard each need a specific role to play to help preserve their mental composure.

Life raft

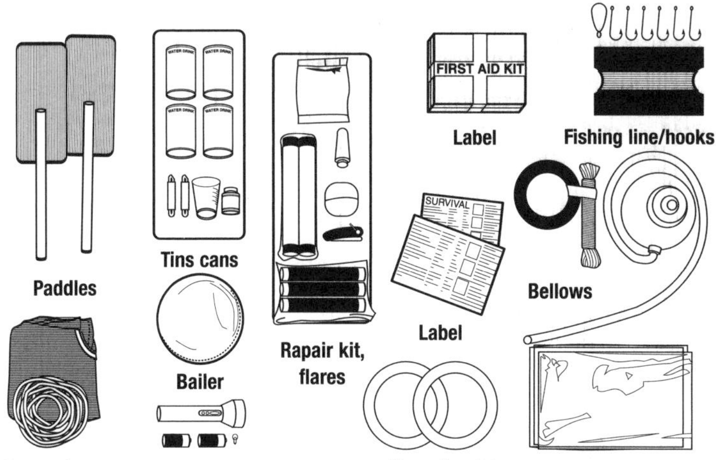

Paddles

Tins cans

Sea anchor

Bailer

Torch

Rapair kit, flares

Label

Label

FIRST AID KIT

Fishing line/hooks

SURVIVAL

Bellows

Resealing lid

Quoit line

Soldiers who suffer from aquaphobia (fear of water) obviously have a problem that needs to be addressed, preferably before they reach basic training. Swimming instructors who specialize in this complaint tend to follow techniques of steady adjustment, the earliest major goal being to get the person to submerge his face and ears in water.

The soldier will, hopefully, come to realize that immersing his head underwater does not lead to a catastrophic influx of water into the nose, ears and mouth. Once the person can accept that fact, it is usually a short step to being a confident swimmer.

Underwater Challenges

Of course, there is a world of difference between a soldier who can swim and a fully fledged combat diver. Combat divers can experience a unique range of mental challenges when operating in deep waters. They have to cope with effects such as high water pressures, low visibility, poor light levels and sound distortion and amplification.

Typical psychological outcomes of these conditions include temporal illusions (mainly that time seems to run quicker than it actually does), reduced visual acuity (peripheral vision tends to be limited) and, on occasions, outright panic. A more serious situation is 'nitrogen narcosis', a physiological condition

Positive signs

Surviving in harsh environments often means looking for the positives rather than the negatives. For example, this view from a life raft could look quite bleak, but the debris, sea birds and cloud formations all indicate that land, and possible rescue, are nearby

US Navy SEALs
Deep-Water Swimming

Deep-water combat diving is one of the most extreme military environments possible. Here, two SEAL divers are deployed from a submarine. They have to cope with the tremendous sense of isolation that often comes with being a human figure in the immensity of an ocean.

experienced typically on dives below 30m (100ft). It produces symptoms similar to extreme intoxication, including confusion, euphoria and carelessness, but can lead to unconsciousness and death if the diver doesn't return to the surface or shallower depths.

Training combat divers for the US Navy SEALs or British Special Boat Service (SBS) involves pressure testing candidates in all manner of high-stress aquatic situations, to weed out those prone to panic. The most important attributes to a combat diver are a steady mind, an exhaustive knowledge of his craft and a meticulous adherence to safety rules.

Depression

While many extreme environments are often exotic and beautiful to look at, they can be hostile places for the psyches of those from more moderate climates. The alien landscape, in which almost everything is utterly unfamiliar, can make a soldier feel a very long way from home, and can precipitate a lasting and debilitating depression.

Depression has a number of contributory causes, including physical, psychological and environmental. It might be precipitated by boredom, long working hours, unfamiliar food, homesickness and danger, but typically it arises from a combination of causes acting adversely on the soldier's mental state. Depression has to be taken seriously by combat leaders. If left unchecked it reduces the efficiency, morale, discipline and motivation of a unit, and can increase undesirable situations such as illegal drug use.

Depression differs from feelings of sadness and 'the blues' by lasting a lot longer, so much so that it has a negative impact on a person's functioning in daily life, including diet, sleep and thought processes. Basic remedies for depression can be as simple as taking more regular exercise, especially challenging aerobic exercise.

Staying as busy as possible is also useful, as it gives you less time to concentrate on your own problems and stops you being isolated. Eating healthy foods could give also provide more energy and give a physical lift.

Treatment

By far the simplest and most effective way of relieving signs of isolation and depression is through talking to someone. Seeking professional help is advised if symptoms are severe, as there may be a chemical imbalance that can be corrected with medication. The third party could be a military psychologist or chaplain, although many soldiers are reluctant to consult these individuals for fear

Despair

The combination of isolation, alienation and being so far from home can have a serious effect on mental health. Keeping busy and avoiding boredom can stave off these negative feelings.

of appearing 'soft' or being taken off active duty. Veteran soldiers, especially veteran NCOs, or supportive friends can therefore be good options.

'Battle Buddies'

The US military operates a beneficial 'buddy' system. Here, a soldier, sailor, airman or Marine is paired with another individual, and together they form a mutually supportive team who look out for each other at all times. By getting to know each other extremely well, furthermore, each buddy is more likely to spot when something is wrong with his partner.

The system promotes morale, teamwork, support and responsibility – not only do you have someone looking out for you, you also have the focus of looking out for them. The buddy system helps to reduce stress and depression, and is known to lower suicide rates. Team-building exercises and rituals also develop empathy and loyalty. The 'Rite of Passage' ceremony at the end of basic training celebrates a trainee becoming a soldier.

Units such as the Marines consider themselves 'Marines for life', and support networks are available for retired Marines who need help. The most important thing about the military community is that there is always going to be someone who feels exactly like you do, and still performs his duties extremely well. You can be reassured that if he can do it, so can you.

Physical symptoms	Mental symptoms	Behavioural symptoms
Fatigue	Anger or irritability	Lack of interest in hobbies
Headaches	Lack of focus	Wanting to be on their own
Digestive complaints	Sadness	Insomnia or sleeping too much
Loss of appetite or weight	Feelings of guilt or worthlessness	Over- or undereating
Increased appetite or weight gain	Nightmares	Increased dependence on tobacco, alcohol or drugs
Lack of energy	Suicidal thoughts	Inability to make decisions

Buddy System

One of the most vital weapons a soldier has is his 'buddy'. Having someone who is constantly looking out for your best interests, both physically and emotionally, makes each individual much stronger. The military community offers life-long loyalty and friends to those accepted into its ranks.

B attle environments can throw you into unfamiliar and harrowing environments, where the sights, sounds, smells and feelings all conspire to disorientate and alarm. In the civilian world, such environments are typically only encountered in something like a severe road accident or disaster situation, and these incidents typically have a fairly limited duration. Being close to or directly involved in sustained combat conditions, especially where there are regular casualties, can be like surviving a serious car accident every day of the week, with all the mental shock that implies.

Another problem comes from the very nature of modern warfare. Peacekeeping duties form a large part of a soldier's role in today's conflicts, as seen in Bosnia, Kosovo and Somalia, where soldiers often spent more time maintaining the (uneasy) peace than in actual combat. It is no longer enough to be physically fit and ready for combat; today's soldier also needs to take on the roles of humanitarian, logistician, crowd controller, negotiator and diplomat. Yet at the same time, we

....

In military life, there are a number of traumatic situations that no amount of training and forethought can prepare you for. Shock can be an inevitable result. However, its negative effects can be minimized by mental strength.

7

The experience of battle can be traumatic. Handling and preventing combat stress reaction (CSR) and post-traumatic stress disorder (PTSD) has therefore become a major issue for modern armed services.

Trauma and Shock

Street Confrontation

Riots are acutely stressful situations for soldiers, as the military personnel are constrained by strict rules of engagement. Strong leadership from officers is paramount to avoid the soldiers opening up with indiscriminate fire.

Clearing Casualties

Casualty evacuation requires a very clear mindset to rise above the emotional trauma of handling wounded comrades. Medical officers need to provide decisive triage, while NCOs should coordinate the evacuation into one smooth effort.

expect our soldiers to switch from peacemakers to fighters in the blink of an eye. They live in what is known as the 'three-block' war, where situations of calm can turn to violence, or even out-and-out war, within the geographical space of three city blocks.

A tragic illustration of this took place on 3 October 1993. The United States was at that time heavily involved in peacekeeping duties in war-ravaged Somalia. In an attempt to control the country's spiralling violence, a team of elite US Rangers and members of Delta Force were sent into the Somali capital, Mogadishu, to apprehend Mohammed Farah Aidid, a local warlord. What was meant to be a 90-minute apprehension operation descended into a 17-hour bloodbath. Following the downing of two Blackhawk helicopters by RPGs, the US team found itself trapped in a nightmarish maze of intricate, claustrophobic streets while hundreds of armed Somali civilians and soldiers opened up on them with automatic weapons. In the chaos that followed, 18 Americans and more than 350 Somalis were killed, and 84 US servicemen were injured. In such situations, it is little wonder that mental scars can last a lifetime.

Stress Build-up
Duration is a critical factor in the development of combat stress.

Research has found that prolonged exposure to combat tends to affect soldiers in predictable ways, based on the number of days in direct action. A soldier deployed into combat for the first time will essentially be on a learning curve for the first 10 days, adjusting to the realities of the experience. For days 10–20, he is at his period of 'maximum efficiency', able to work at his optimum of tactical awareness and confidence.

After 30 days of exposure to combat, however, this efficiency begins a marked dip, at first through overconfidence (and a corresponding increase in the likelihood of becoming a casualty) and then descending into emotional exhaustion around the 40-day mark. By 60 days in continuous action, the soldier can even plunge into a vegetative state, suffering from complete mental breakdown.

Naturally, military commanders aim to rotate units out of combat duties every few days or so – this is critical to the mental health of the men – but long-range weaponry means that enemies can reach out and touch units even when they are deployed within a base. Soldiers in Afghanistan and Iraq have experienced mortar, IED and RPG attacks on an almost daily basis, and frontline US troops in Vietnam during the 1960s and early 1970s could be involved in firefights, on varying scales, almost every day of their deployment.

Almost all soldiers will experience intense fear during combat, and an adrenalin 'dump' unlike anything they have ever experienced before. There can be positive benefits here. Fear can give you an edge, keeping you alert and focused and hyper-vigilant for threats. It can also provide you with the energy to keep going even when exhausted. However, if fear and extreme awareness have to be maintained over a long period of time, what started as an alert mind can soon slip into an exhausted one.

Combat Stress Reaction

The threat to soldiers' minds is now known as Combat Stress Reaction (CSR), or, according to more modern US terminology, Combat and Operational Stress Reaction (COSR). CSR covers a range of psychological conditions and symptoms that vary considerably between individuals. The clinical community makes an interesting divide in symptoms, known as 'underload' and 'overload'. When performing at optimum level, the mind is moderately aroused, alert, attentive and calm in any situation (the ideal state of mind for a Special Forces soldier during combat). When in 'underload', one is inattentive, distracted, uninterested, suffers low initiative and feels depressed.

Combat Stress

Feeling unable to cope in certain situations is one of the many symptoms of combat stress, often accmpanied by anger, depression and confusion. Being aware of the symptoms can make CSR easier to spot in both yourself and others.

PHYSICAL	EMOTIONAL	BEHAVIOuRAL
• Constant movement	• Anxiety	• Indecisiveness
• Severe startle response	• Grief	• Inattention
• Shaking or trembling	• Inability to concentrate	• Carelessness
• Weakness and paralysis	• Nightmares	• Hyper-alertness
• Impaired vision, hearing and touch (loss of sensation)	• Self doubt	• Lack of motivation
	• Anger	• Irritability
• Total exhaustion	• Excessive concern with minor issues	• Lack of initiative
• Immobility		• Tears, crying
• Stares vacantly	• Loss of confidence in self and unit	• Inability to relax
• Acute abdominal pain		• Argumentative
• Impaired speech or muteness		
• Staggers or sways		
• Heart palpitations		
• Hyperventilation		
• Insomnia or severe sleep disturbance		

www.behavioralhealth.army.mil/provider/combatstress.html

'Overload' is the opposite: judgement is impaired, the mind is over-stimulated, tense and agitated, and attention is fragmented. Neither state of mind is healthy for a soldier in combat, especially when important decisions need to be made quickly.

The US Army Medical Department defines the symptoms of CSR according to physical, emotional and behavioural categories, indicating how CSR can possess the soldier's whole being. In its extreme forms, CSR expresses itself as above.

CSR, and its grim companion, post-traumatic stress disorder (PTSD), have reached almost epidemic proportions in recent years. The US Army, for example, diagnosed 76,176 cases of PTSD between 2000 and 2011. CSR has been implicated in several high-profile atrocities, such as the alleged killing of 16 Afghan civilians in Kandahar on 11 March 2011 by Staff Sergeant Robert Bales. A high-ranking US officer told *The New York Times:* 'When it all comes out,

it will be a combination of stress, alcohol and domestic issues – he just snapped.'

Preventing CSR

While a soldier can never be fully prepared for live combat until he has experienced it for real, military

Sharing Experiences

Talking through difficult situations or fears can help you to put them in perspective. While this is often easier in civilian life than in military life, it can reduce the negative effects of stress on both the individual and the unit.

US Forces Stress Management Techniques

- Assure every effort is made to provide for the troops' welfare.
- Instil confidence in each Service member and his equipment, unit and leadership.
- Be decisive and assertive; demonstrate competence and fair leadership.
- Provide sleep and/or rest, especially during continuous operations, whenever possible.
- Ensure sleep for decision-making personnel.
- Set realistic goals for progressive development of the individual and team.
- Systematically test the achievement of these goals.
- Recognize that battle duration and intensity increase stress.
- Be aware of environmental stressors such as light level, temperature and precipitation.
- Recognize that individuals and units react differently to the same stress.
- Learn the signs of stress in yourself and others.
- Recognize that fear is a normal part of combat stress.
- Rest minor stress casualties briefly, keeping them with their unit.
- Be aware of background stress sources prior to combat, such as family concerns and/or separation, economic problems, etc.
- Provide an upward, downward and lateral information flow to minimize stress due to a lack of communication.
- Practice stress control through cross training, task allocation, tasks matching and task sharing.
- Look for stress signs and a decreased ability to tolerate stress.
- Practice and master stress-coping techniques.
- Face combat stress; it is unhealthy to deny the stresses of combat.

– FM 6–22.5 'Combat Stress'

training (covered in more detail in Chapter 4) goes a long way towards building up prior resilience, fortitude and experience, and if done well it serves to 'battleproof' soldiers against the worst effects of combat stress. The more realistic training is, and the more often it is repeated, the better equipped soldiers are to adjust when they experience combat for real. To this end, forces such as the Marines spend more than 80 per cent of their training time on practical field exercises.

Highly trained forces are also more likely to remain calm during battle and less likely to suffer adverse effects after battle. Training using live rounds in realistic surroundings minimizes the shock of confronting real bullets in combat for the first time. Interestingly, despite often experiencing the most stressful combat situations, rates of CSR are much less common among the elite forces, in part because of their rigorous training programmes.

Fortunately, there has been a huge amount of work put into studying how to minimize CSR among soldiers in the field. The Army Medical Department mentioned above has distributed a useful acronym for remembering the core principles of stress management: brevity, immediacy, contact, expectancy, proximity and simplicity (BICEPS). These treatment principles break down as follows:

Brevity For the early onset of CSR, the soldier should be given one to three days of rest near to the frontline. Any more than this runs of risk of the soldier mentally detaching himself from his duties and developing an increasing fear of going back to service. If the CSR is severe, however, the soldier will be passed on to psychiatric services further removed from the battlefront, or even sent home.

Immediacy Leaders should put in place CSR reduction measures as soon as the symptoms appear; delay in implementing these measures can mean that the behaviours become more entrenched.

Contact 'The Soldier must be encouraged to continue to think of himself as a war-fighter, rather than a patient or a sick person', notes the AMD. This also means that the soldier's unit needs to stay in regular contact, so the soldier feels that he is still a valued member of a team and isn't being judged for his absence.

Expectancy The soldier will be told that his symptoms are normal and that he is expected to make a full recovery. Expectancy, it should be noted, is about optimism and not a coercive attitude towards returning a man or woman to duty.

Proximity Soldiers suffering from CSR should be kept close to the frontline, but never held in aid stations alongside physical casualties. By staying near the frontline, the soldier retains a mental interest in his unit and the unfolding action.

Simplicity This refers to a range of straightforward treatment techniques that can have an immediate positive effect on reducing CSR. They are given as follows:

- reassure of normality (normalize the reaction)
- rest (respite from combat or break from work)
- replenish bodily needs (such as thermal comfort, water, food, hygiene and sleep).
- restore confidence with purposeful activities and talk
- retain contact with fellow soldiers and unit

By following these procedures, CSR can be tackled early on, preventing it from growing into something with serious long-term implications. Their implementation, of course, depends on good leaders who take CSR seriously. Not all officers are as enlightened, believing that mental breakdown is purely a sign of weakness. Thankfully, such attitudes are steadily disappearing. Officers must operate as supportive leaders, recognizing the unique stresses of combat and ensuring that all members of the unit watch out for each other.

A Team Mind

One of the most important ways of strengthening mental endurance during combat is to be a member of a united, cohesive team. The elite forces encourage a strong team identity, with high levels of tactical, technological and emotional inter-reliance. Each individual needs to contribute to unit confidence, ensuring that there are no weak points that might endanger the unit.

It is not for nothing that teams with a powerful shared identity regularly perform at a much higher level than units that are disconnected or less motivated. Examples of this in action are numerous, particularly when highly trained, highly motivated regular armed forces fight against poorly trained, socially alienated conscript armies. During the invasion of Iraq in 2003, US, British and coalition forces, with their lower ranks trained to take battlefield initiative, often defeated far larger enemy units, which were on the whole centralized on the officer class (meaning the unit lost its direction once an officer was killed) and had received inadequate training.

If individuals share tough training regimes, they are immediately united by their experiences. This also gives them a chance to practice working as a team under stressful, uncertain conditions. Take this into a combat situation and the mutual experiences keep growing, even if the group shares something as personal as the loss of a team member. The optimum group size is thought to be three to

Teamwork

The most proficient military teams stand together during training and live combat. Teamwork builds trust in one another, which in turn helps to reassure soldiers in the face of trauma and shock.

eight men, with elite force teams rarely working in groups larger than 10.

Many studies carried out during and after the Korean War confirmed these theories. The teams that performed especially well often had shared levels of motivation, discipline, sociability, aspirations and loyalty. They were confident of their individual merits and of their place within the team. As the US Navy SEALs say: 'There is no "I" in team or SEAL.'

Torture and Captivity

A particular harrowing cause of mental trauma such as PTSD is being held captive or suffering from torture. While this might be an unlikely scenario, the fact remains that Special Forces troops are likely to enter extremely hostile enemy territory, which means that the chance of being caught or captured increases.

As described in the 2002 *Antiterrorism Personal Protection Guide*, while the enemy's aim may be to kill US soldiers, there can also be value in taking hostages:

> *US military personnel captured by terrorists or detained by hostile foreign governments are often held for individual exploitation, to influence the US Government, or both. This exploitation can take many forms, but each form*

Rough Treatment

A soldier endures physical abuse at the hands of his captors and civilian crowds. In such a situation, minimize the physical danger by keeping your head tucked downwards and shoulders hunched. Avoid confrontational behaviour and eye contact.

Extreme Trauma

'Fake' shootings may be carried out on prisoners in front of you for intimidation or to get information. There is no avoiding the trauma of such events, but the soldier has to avoid dwelling constantly on the threats.

of exploitation is designed to assist the foreign government or the terrorist captors. In the past, terrorists or governments exploited detainees for information and propaganda efforts, including confessions to crimes never committed. This assisted or lent credibility to the detainer. Governments also have been exploited in such situation to make damaging statements about themselves or to force them to appear weak in relation to other governments. Governments have paid ransoms for captives of terrorists and such payments have improved terrorist finances, supplies, status and operations, often prolonging the terror carried on by such groups. The US Government's policy is that it will not negotiate with terrorists.
– CJCS Guide 5260, *Antiterrorism Personal Protection Guide* (2002)

Reasons for taking POWs change with each major conflict. During World War II, an astonishing 5.7 million Soviets were taken prisoner by the German Army, who built POW and work camps for holding them and working them to death. Levels of POWs were also high in the Indochina War, the Vietnam War and the Gulf War, among other conflicts throughout history.

However, the rise in terrorist cells and insurgent groups who capture a single soldier for a very specific purpose has changed the game somewhat. Captives may be used as a tool to bargain for political prisoners, to obtain money or weapons, to raise the profile of a group or agenda, or for propaganda purposes. In addition, a harsh reality is that terrorists simply take military prisoners to make examples of them. Terrorist cells such as al-Qaeda have taken hostages with the express purpose of torturing and killing them, footage of which is then released to the world's media via the internet.

As with several major stresses of military life, it is the utter lack of control over your own situation and life during captivity that is hard to take. You are at the whim of others, who may have a specific political agenda that you are as yet unaware of. Even such basic activities as eating, sleeping or going to the toilet may be up to someone else, who may or may not enjoy seeing others suffer.

Held Captive
The most dangerous period for a POW is the first few hours following capture. It is during this time that you are just as likely to be killed as to be taken to a prison camp or terrorist cell, unless the kidnappers have a specific reason for holding a hostage.

Held Captive

Being held captive is a frightening descent into powerlessness. However, staying alert and gathering as much information as you can about your captors and surroundings can be empowering, giving you at least the hope of escape.

If you are captured by an enemy or taken hostage by terrorists, avoid defiance or aggression towards your captors.

Instead, act with obedience and deference (however difficult this may initially be for you), don't make eye contact, follow any orders you are given and speak only in response to questions in a calm tone of voice. Your aim is to give as little as possible away about yourself and to avoid drawing little special attention to yourself.

Even if you appear compliant, the inner workings of your mind can boil with defiance. One of your first priorities is to use all your senses to find out as much as you can about your captors and situation. Any knowledge or understanding you can gain as to why you are being taken hostage, where you are going or what might happen to you can be crucial. Ask yourself questions such as:

- Who appears to be the leader of the group? Who is second-in-command?
- What is your location? Mentally take note of any prominent landmarks or street names around you – being able to identify this location might come in useful later on during a rescue or escape attempt.
- From the conversation among the captors, can you pick up any details about where you are being taken? Even if you

don't speak the language, listen out for any familiar place names or regularly repeated words that sound significant.

- Do any of your captors appear to have physical or mental weaknesses, such as leg injuries or experience of bullying by other members of the group, that you might be able to exploit later on? Conversely, these characteristics might also pose a danger to you, so they are useful to note.

Sharing any information with fellow hostages can also be useful, so do so while you get the chance – prisoners are often separated so that they cannot plan a joint escape or concoct stories that coincide. However, do be aware that informers may be planted within a group of prisoners with the aim of discovering as much about you and your organization's purpose as possible. Avoid volunteering personal facts whenever possible, while taking in every piece of information about your surroundings that you can.

If you have a skill that might make you more useful in the eyes of your captors, use it to your advantage by providing service to prison staff. This may jar, especially if fellow hostages are mistreated in front of you, but escape or survival must be your aims. Take care, however, not to

Solitary Confinement

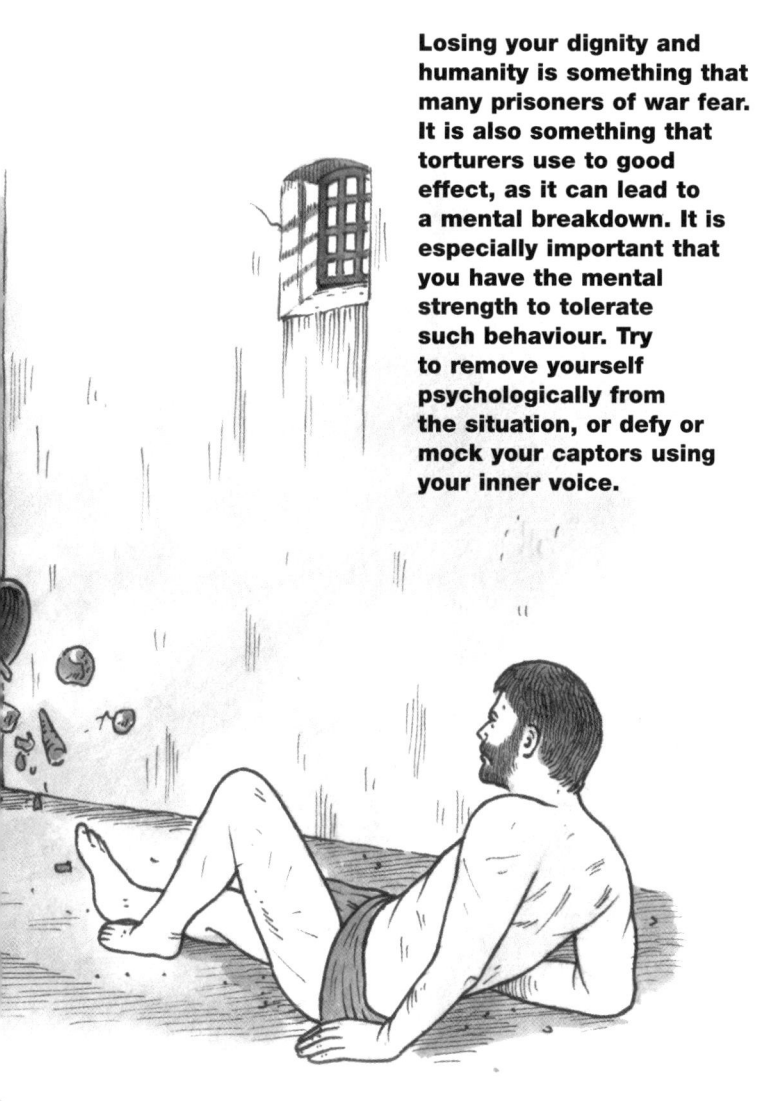

Losing your dignity and humanity is something that many prisoners of war fear. It is also something that torturers use to good effect, as it can lead to a mental breakdown. It is especially important that you have the mental strength to tolerate such behaviour. Try to remove yourself psychologically from the situation, or defy or mock your captors using your inner voice.

Sensory Deprivation

This prisoner is being kept isolated, dressed in a hooded garment, goggles and ear defenders so that he is unable to see or hear anything. This form of sensory deprivation completely disorientates the captive, making him unlikely to know how long he has been in captivity and increasing his dependence on his captors.

enter a situation where you are required to give away information or inform on fellow prisoners. It is hard to maintain morals and standards when you are desperate. At these times, remember that you are a soldier and act with dignity, no matter what anyone else is doing. Your actions may have consequences that live with you for the rest of your life.

While it may be utterly abhorrent to try to build a relationship with your captors, doing so can provide you with information relevant to making an escape, or give you a protector against more physical guards. Stick to what you know is common ground. You will both feel similar physical sensations of hunger, cold or thirst. Key issues to avoid are religion or politics, topics that could lead to serious disagreements and even more serious repercussions for you. Such discussions will only serve to highlight the distance between you and your captors. It may also anger your captors and remind them of what he is fighting for. Do not let yourself become the embodiment of evil or heresy that your captor so despises.

The condition of 'Stockholm Syndrome' (often a result of long-term captivity, where the captive bonds with his or her captor as their only companion or link to the outside world) must be avoided – you cannot allow your loyalties to become divided, so never let yourself forget what and who you are fighting for.

Staving Off Boredom

One of the hardest things to overcome during long-term captivity (when the fear has subsided) is boredom. Weeks or even months can pass with nothing happening to vary the routine. One of the most important things you can do is to remind yourself (and others) of life outside the prison. You are not just a nameless, faceless, forgotten person. You have a family, friends, interests, beliefs and skills that are uniquely your own, and you will always have these things.

Establish your own routine (in addition to the one that might be imposed upon you), as it allows you to regain control. The routine could include running through information in your head, such as song lyrics, film or book plots, or making plans for the future.

Imagining practical activities in 'real-time' can be another useful way of staving off boredom and depression. If your plans involve training to be a pilot, for example, run as many details as you can through your head as if you were actually doing it (the visualization training described in Chapter 4 can help with this). Add as much detail to your real-time mental activities as you can, such as the weather, what

Boredom

Boredom can be one of the hardest things to endure in prolonged captivity, especially if you are isolated. It is important to keep your mind occupied with mental challenges, problem-solving activities (which could be related to plotting your escape) and creating imaginary worlds (as long as you don't lose touch with reality). Trying to find common ground with one of your captors, such as family or sports, can also help pass the time. Be careful however, that you guard against giving away personal information.

Torture

Shown here are various forms of torture, including isolation, physical and verbal force, and exposure to extreme noise. Such harsh techniques, especially when mixed with good treatment or the promise of release, can cause many to reach their breaking point.

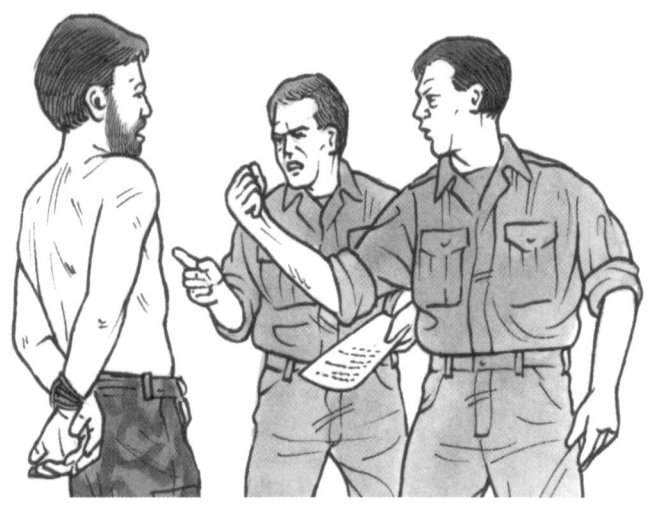

you had for breakfast and how you felt as you successfully landed the plane.

Another useful pastime can be creating imaginary stories, situations or worlds, but do not let yourself replace your reality with fantasy. Staying mindful means you will remain motivated, physically fit and not relax and give out important information. However, sometimes

boredom can be broken in a most unpleasant way, and it is here, especially, that you need to be on your guard.

Interrogation and Torture
If you are subject to interrogation, the only personal information you may traditionally release is your name, rank, serial number, date of

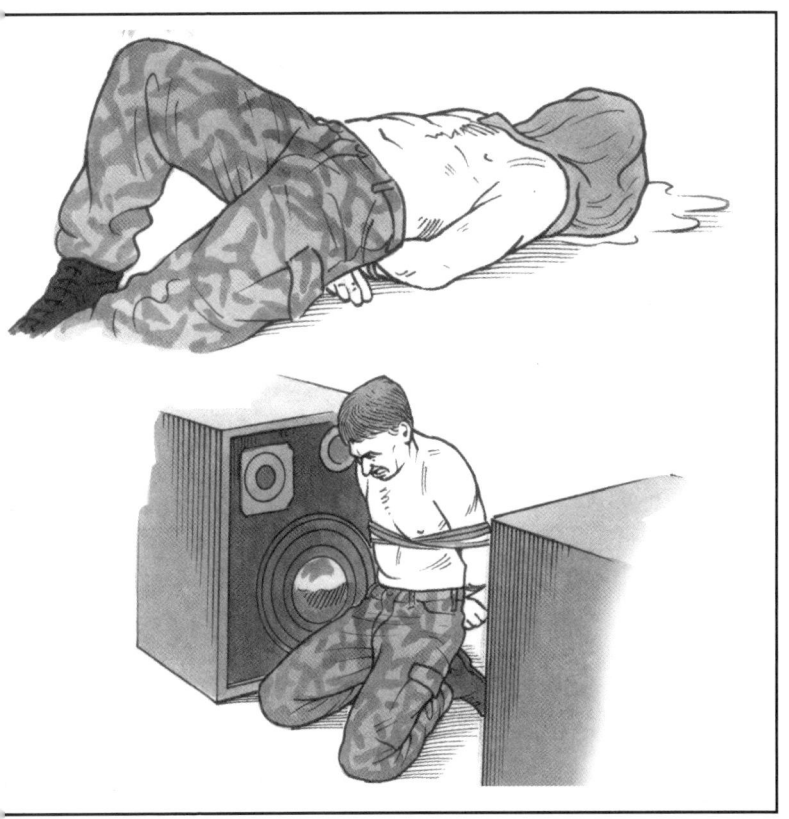

birth and – if it isn't privileged information – the circumstances surrounding your capture. Avoid any discussion on military service, facts about locations or numbers of personnel or anything you may know about future operations. If discussions become chatty, even friendly, be careful that you aren't being lulled into a false sense of security. Good interrogators can extract useful information from the most banal comments, so always be guarded in what you say.

If you continue to withstand interrogation, mental and physical torture may be applied. This can involve long periods of isolation, brutal beatings, being forced into stress positions or confined spaces,

Escaping Captivity

An opportunistic escape, such as the one shown here, may be the only chance you have to escape. Such an endeavour should only be attempted if you are sure that your captors are fully distracted.

starvation, sleep deprivation and more medieval horrors.

Any mental strength you can draw upon in between the episodes of torture can help, such as meditation and visualization, which allow you to escape temporarily from your situation and give you some degree of control. You may also draw strength from the knowledge that the longer you hold out, the less harm can be done to your comrades.

Note, however, that under prolonged torture, even the toughest of characters can crack. If you do, and find yourself talking to spare yourself intolerable pain, try at least to give information that is non-consequential to the enemy or which you know will be out of date. Such minor acts of defiance can be enormously empowering.

Escape Strategies

Attempting to escape from captivity is always an incredibly risky option, yet it should be your primary goal. While some escape attempts require lots of planning, preparation and gathering supplies, sometimes taking advantage of a sudden distraction is your best bet. For the highest chances of success, the best time to attempt an escape is actually in the first few hours – or even moments – after capture. The initial confusion of seizing a hostage can be just as disorientating for the captors, especially if they had not expected this turn of events. During this time, any advantage or distraction should be seized, such as nearby firefights, to attempt your escape. Quick, decisive action is needed here, as you may only have seconds to act.

The sooner you manage to escape, the more mentally and physically fit you will be, thereby increasing your chances of survival on the run. In contrast, the longer you spend in captivity, the more your physical strength will deteriorate. Build exercise into your daily routine if possible, varying it for interest and to keep all muscle groups fit. Try to practise team sports – if your captors allow – as these can boost morale while surreptitiously allowing you to develop fitness (too much solitary training can be a sign that you are preparing for something).

Your escape plan, if methodically prepared, should be as simple as possible and make allowance for things not going as intended. Basically look for any ways you can take advantage of routines or infrastructural weak points in your prison camp or building. Have a clear idea of where you will go and what you will do outside the prison walls; history has many examples of prisoners escaping only to be captured within days of being on the run.

Ensure that you collect or make survival gear and appropriate clothing, as the environment will also be your enemy on the outside. If you

Dealing with the Fallen

The death of a fellow soldier can be one of the worst events that military personnel have to experience. Survivor's guilt can be especially difficult to overcome. What is important is that the soldier focuses as much on the future as on the past, and relies on his surviving comrades to cope with the loss.

can, avoid using violence against guards (or their guard dogs, for that matter) as part of your escape; such actions will make your enemy far less forgiving if things go wrong and you are recaptured.

After the Battle

The mental shift from active combat to peacetime or back to civilian life can

be tough. Suddenly, all the priorities and routines change. You are no longer part of a team with a shared goal, but need to be completely self-sufficient to support yourself and any dependents. There are many psychological problems that can come with life after combat, including depression, nightmares, insomnia, substance or alcohol abuse, self-harm or even suicide attempts. Of course, not everyone will suffer such extreme reactions, and many can return to civilian life with the added pride and self-confidence of knowing how well they conducted themselves during battle. However, it is unlikely that living through sustained combat will have no effect on your mental health, even if it is only in the form of survivor's guilt –

that you made it through while many others did not.

Post-traumatic Stress Disorder

PTSD is a mental condition precipitated directly by a traumatic experience, such as serious injury, witnessing violent death, narrowly surviving being killed and handling the loss of friends. For many combat soldiers, the damage caused by exposure to trauma can be extreme and have long-term effects. In fact, one of the ways of diagnosing PTSD is longevity – symptoms must have lasted more than one month. They must also have caused considerable impairment in lifestyle or ability to function, which may worsen over time.

The symptoms of PTSD may not appear straight away, and may come and go, but they typically include:

- Reliving or re-experiencing, where the traumatic event is replayed in the mind constantly, both in flashbacks and nightmares.
- Avoidance, where anything connected to or recalling the traumatic event is avoided, even talking or thinking about it.
- Numbing, in which all interests or emotions are suppressed (both negative ones that remind the casualty of the event, and positive ones that he may feel guilty for having).
- Arousal or hyperarousal, where the casualty is always jumpy, nervous and tense, as if he is

Inactivity

Soldiers suffering from CSR need to avoid isolating themselves from the outside world, and spending too much time in their own thoughts. Purposeful activity and an outward-looking attitude can go a long way to helping overcome trauma, although more specialist treatments are often required in support.

waiting for a threat or something bad to happen.

Prolonged, untreated PTSD can lead to further symptoms, such as

depression, physical pains, fatigue, difficulty or inability to hold down a job, risky behaviour such as gambling or fighting, relationship troubles, domestic violence and dependence on alcohol or drugs. The trigger of the traumatic event can also be just part of the problem, where all your fears and self-doubts and inability to act become caught up in the

Reunion

When a soldier is reunited with his family after a long deployment, the experience can be emotionally overwhelming. What the soldier needs to adjust to is the reality of civilian life, which can often seem frustrating, boring and purposeless after the intensity of combat. In essence, he needs to give as much effort to peace as he did to war.

memory. Suppressing your feelings or hoping they will go away on their own is the worst thing you can do.

Prevention

Prevention is naturally far better than cure, and many of the steps for tackling CSR outlined above are relevant to the prevention of PTSD. The key with PTSD is that the sooner disorders are diagnosed, the less harm they can do. A psychological debriefing as soon as possible after the traumatic event – which gives the individual the opportunity to express his feelings – can be of benefit, as it aims to reduce immediate stress and give people an outlet for their emotions. The casualty should try to talk about the event from his point of view, including how it felt, with someone he trusts. At the very least, he should take a few moments to write down what happened from his point of view, again including how he felt and what he did.

Looking back on this at a later stage may help him to realize that he did everything he could under the circumstances. Advice on how to control anxiety and promote calmness can also help. Medicinal treatments include administering cortisol hormones after the traumatic event; the hormone is often lower in people who are prone to PTSD, so increasing levels can reduce the negative effects of stress.

Talking Treatments

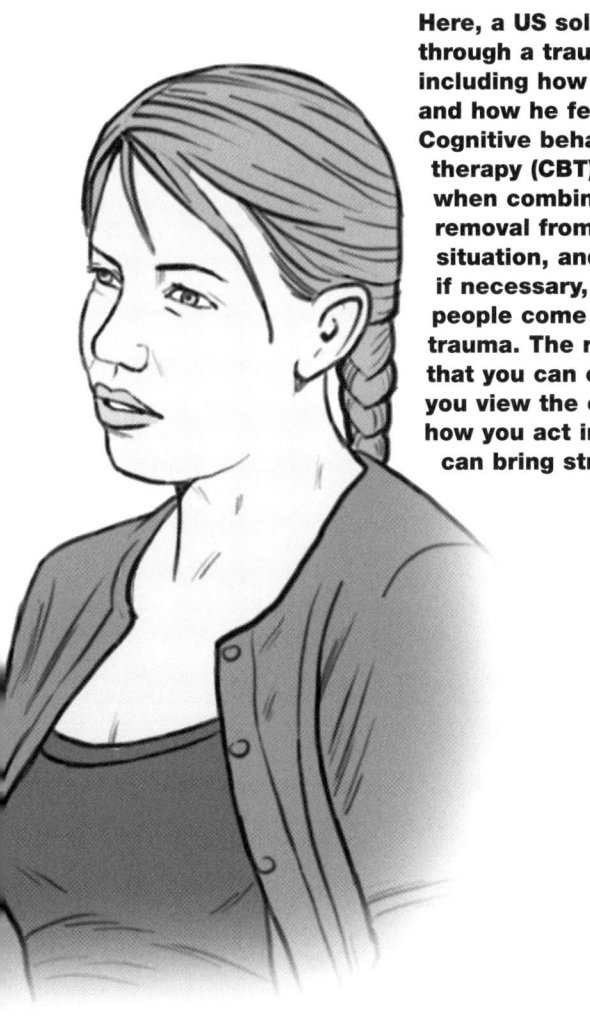

Here, a US soldier talks through a traumatic event, including how he reacted and how he felt afterwards. Cognitive behavioural therapy (CBT), especially when combined with removal from the stressful situation, and medication if necessary, can help people come to terms with trauma. The realization that you can control how you view the event and how you act in the future can bring strength.

Treatments

Treatments for PTSD are available and have a high rate of success in alleviating symptoms altogether. You must ensure that you get a diagnosis from a medical professional so that treatment is suitable for your individual condition. The most common forms of treatment for PTSD are psychotherapy or counselling, medication or a combination of both treatments:

Psychotherapy This most often takes the form of cognitive behavioural therapy (CBT), which is a preferred treatment by the US Department of Defense. This form of therapy aims to use a systematic approach to replace negative behaviours or responses for positive ones. CBT helps individuals to identify and gradually face up to harmful, upsetting thoughts or emotions – anything that reminds them of the traumatic event – and to replace these thoughts with more constructive ones.

Sensory association has a very powerful effect, so any sounds, sights or smells, such as loud traffic, flashing lights or blood, may trigger unwanted emotions that take you back to the traumatic event. There is no way to avoid all of these triggers in everyday life (unless you remain inside all day and do not see anyone, which can be symptoms of PTSD sufferers), so exposure therapy is used to reduce the effect of these triggers, and to stop them having such a strong association with the trauma. The systematic approach comes from building up this exposure, so that eventually the casualty can think and talk about the trauma calmly, even in a place or situation that reminds him of it.Understanding that you cannot change the past, but do have power over your future, brings control back to the individual.

Medication Selective serotonin reuptake inhibitors (SSRIs), such as Prozac, have been found to be effective in the treatment of PTSD. They are often used to treat depression and anxiety, and work by increasing the levels of serotonin in your brain (serotonin aids good moods and feelings of well-being). This can make you feel more positive about past events and the future, and can enable some people to carry on with their lives until they feel ready to stop taking the drugs. SSRIs – or any prescription medication – should only be taken on the advice of a medical professional. Check the possible side effects before taking any medication.

For many people, combining medication with therapy has the highest rate of successful recovery. Medication may make you feel better more quickly, but the underlying cause of the problem is not being addressed.

New Challenges

The most severe challenge a soldier can face is that of loss of limbs, especially after the active military lifestyle. Yet the same courage, tenacity and focus required for combat will also provide the seeds of a new future.

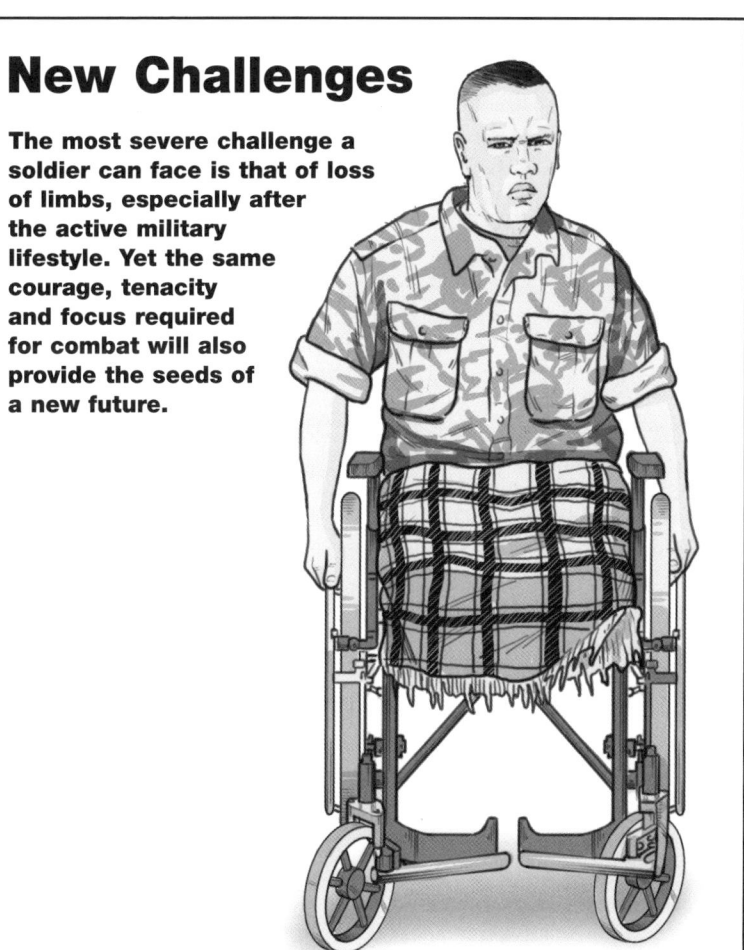

Therefore, as soon as you stop taking the medication, your symptoms may reccur unless they are treated through counselling. Awareness and treatment of military mental disorders are constantly improving. Never feel that you cannot talk to anyone or ask for help if you need it.

Appendices

Appendix 1: Combat First Aid

Although space here does not allow a study of practical combat first aid (which is typically the province of medics), having a decent grasp of the basics can help you to handle the trauma of dealing with seriously injured people.

If you act ineffectively when handling a wounded comrade, this scenario will likely come back to haunt you after the event, particularly if the casualty is permanently disabled in some way or dies. With many fatal combat wounds there is often little a first-aider can do to save the person, but understanding some basic medical procedures will help you either save a life or recognize why your couldn't.

Keep Calm
Keeping calm and remaining in control of a situation is always important, and never more so than in the presence of casualties. What will help you is to have a few basic and important medical procedures in your mental toolbox to give you clarity of action. If such medical instruction isn't provided to you within your basic training, attend any good first aid course or gain some insight from a platoon or company medic.

Familiarity with these techniques means that you will perform them more readily and with greater confidence, helping you to prolong life until medical services arrive at the scene.

Memory Techniques
Use memory devices to help you recall basic medical treatments in high-stress situations. For example, every injured person, especially if he is unconscious or unresponsive, should have his vital functions checked, as denoted by the 'ABC' mnemonic.

Performing Triage
Another challenge you might find in a casualty situation is performing triage. This involves ranking casualties according to their priority of treatment, and it is no easy matter. One casualty might be screaming with pain, but the screams at least denote that he is breathing, conscious and has a heartbeat. Someone who is lying quietly in a corner, apparently unconscious and with only shallow breathing and a thin pulse, probably requires your more urgent attention.

Various official categories of triage have been devised to help

Compressing a Wound

First aid is not complicated to learn, but gives you the confidence to handle basic wounds. For example, applying downward pressure to a wound compresses damaged blood vessels, reducing the flow of blood and promoting clotting at the wound site. Be prepared to maintain the pressure for many minutes.

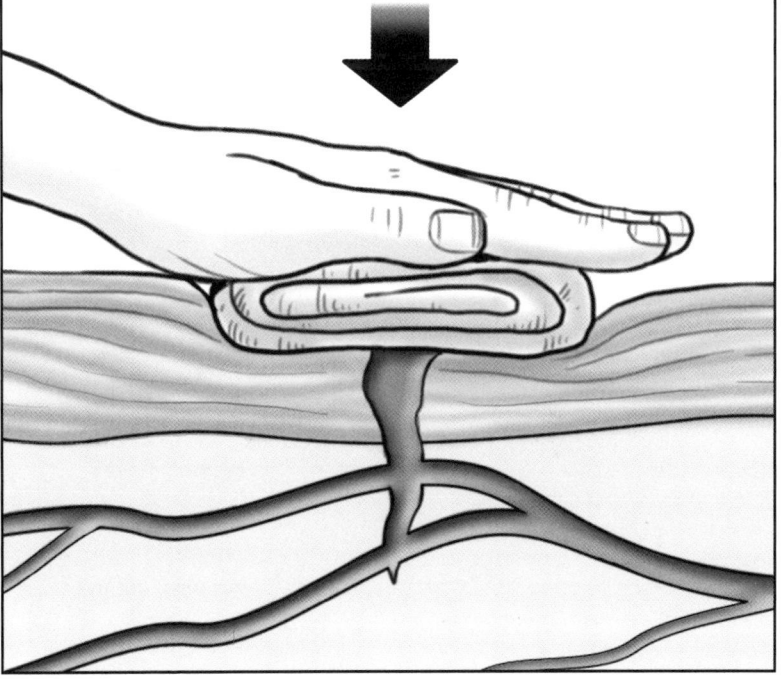

the medic or doctor streamline his or her triage decisions. Those recommended by the US Army, with their civilian equivalents, are listed below, on page 301.

Applying these categories to a mass of wounded people requires a very dispassionate mindset if correct decisions are to be made. In these situations, imagine you

Performing Triage

Triage is the process of grading casualties according to the severity of their injuries, and prioritizing medical treatment accordingly. The mental challenge for medics is to be extremely strict in their judgements, basing their assessments purely on the medical information and not on any other considerations, such as their personal relationship with the victims.

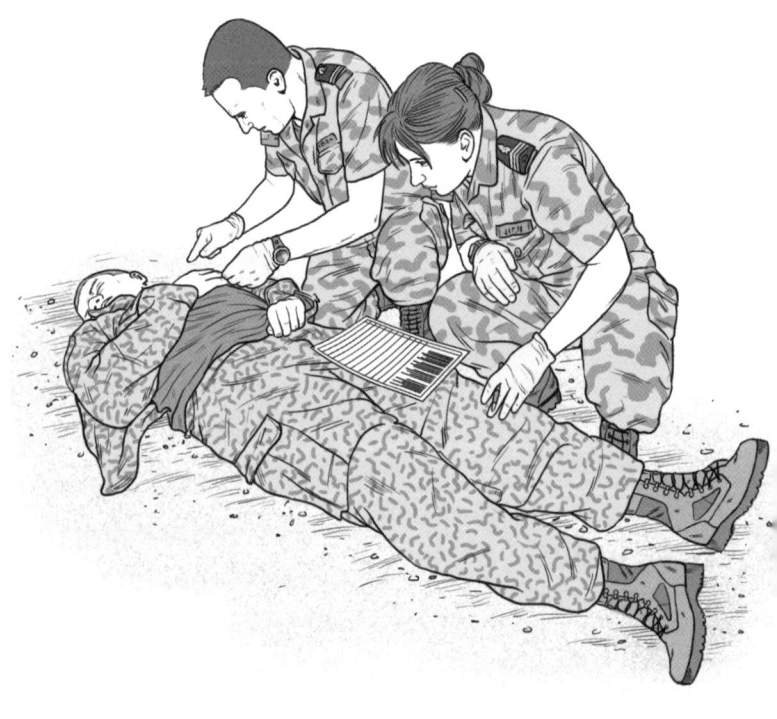

Triage tags

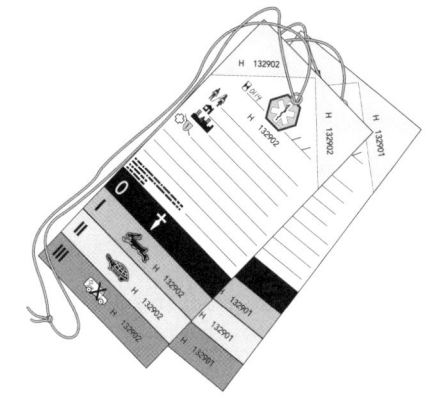

Triage Category: Combat Setting	Triage Category: Civilian Setting	Category Description
Immediate	Critical	This group includes those who require lifesaving surgery. The surgical procedures in this category should not be time consuming and should concern only those patients with high chances of survival.
Delayed	Urgent	This group includes casualties who are badly in need of time-consuming surgery, but whose general condition permits delay in surgical treatment without unduly endangering life. Sustained treatment will be required.
Minimal	Minor	These casualties have relatively minor injuries and can effectively care for themselves or can be helped by non-medical personnel. Care can be delayed for hours to days.
Expectant	Catastrophic	Casualties in this category have wounds that are so extensive that even if they were the sole casualty and had the benefit of optimal medical resource application, their survival would be unlikely.

– US Army Combined Arms Centre, http://usacac.army.mil/cac2/call/docs/06-08/ap-b.asp

are a computer, analyzing the facts and coming to a decision on that basis only. Remind yourself that seemingly hard attitudes towards those in the 'Expectant' category are vital if those in the 'Immediate' category are to survive.

Bandaging a Wound

When bandaging a bleeding wound, tie a thick, sterile pad in place over the injury with a long bandage, the knot of the bandage away from the pad. Do not tie the bandage so tightly that it affects circulation in the limb.

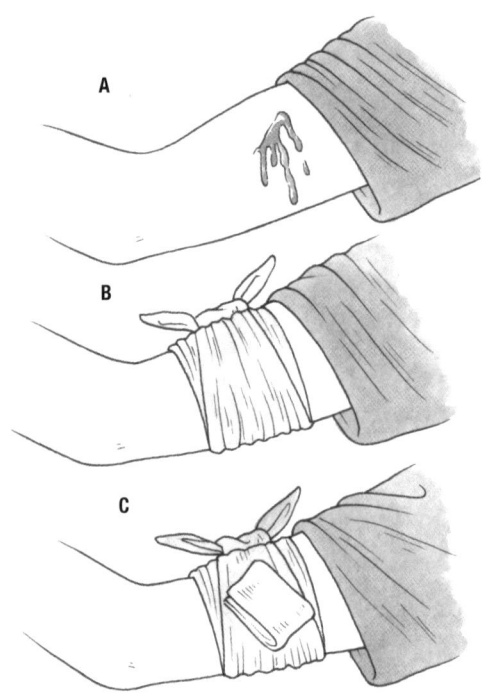

Combat is a uniquely traumatic experience. Recognizing this fact, and accepting that human beings don't have a limitless ability to cope, should form the basis of sound military policy, aimed at keeping service people mentally healthy for the duration of their lives.

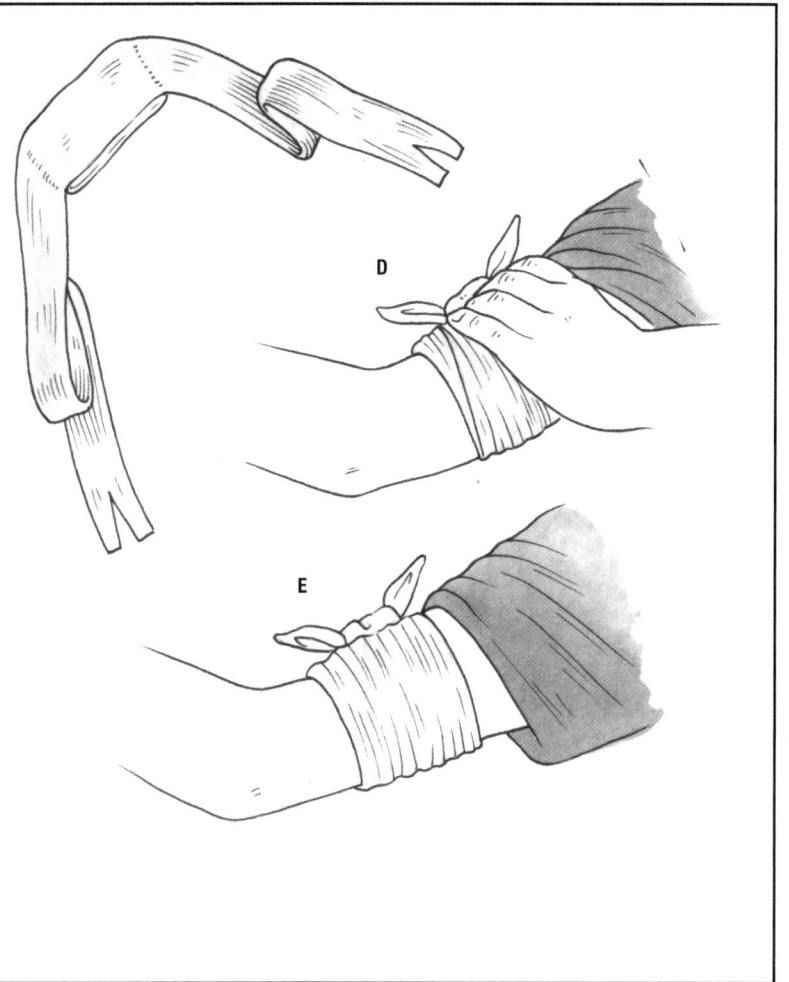

ABC

A – Airway Checking first for signs of neck injuries, gently tilt the head backwards and lift the chin so that the airway is clear. Next, open the mouth and look for any visible obstructions, such as the tongue, foreign bodies or vomit, removing/clearing any that you see.

B – Breathing Assess breathing by placing your cheek next to the casualty's nose and mouth to listen or feel for breath. Feel the chest for signs of it rising and falling. You should feel or see signs of 12–30 breaths a minute. If there are no signs of breathing after 10 seconds, administer artificial respiration.

C – Circulation Once airways and breathing have been checked, feel for a pulse (using your fingers as they have no pulse of their own). Hold the outer edge of the casualty's wrist or feel the throat on either side of the windpipe. If there is no pulse, administer cardio-pulmonary resuscitation.

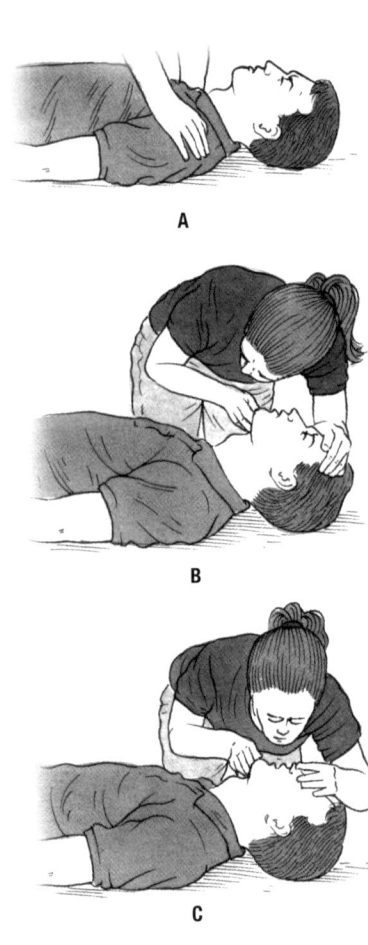

A

B

C

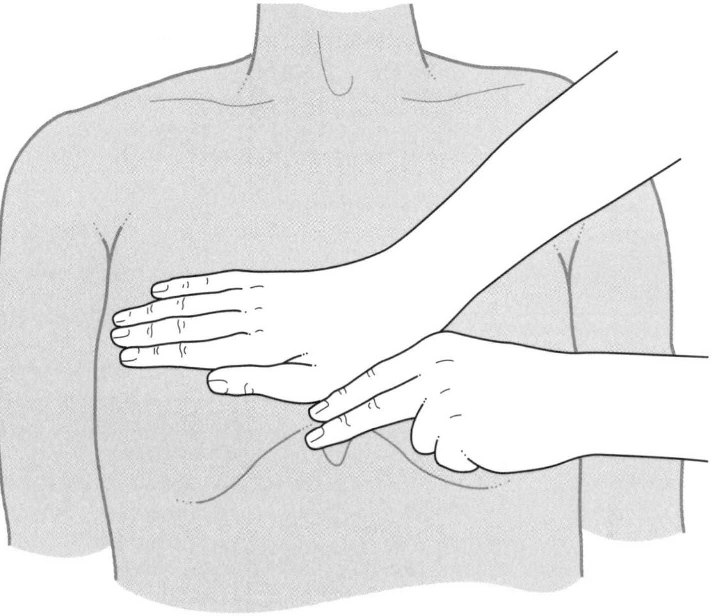

Finding the right spot for delivering CPR compressions

Checking the pulse

Chest compressions

Appendix 2
US Army Classifications of Combat Stress Reaction Effects

Mild Stress Reactions		
Physical	**Emotional**	**Behavioural**
• Fatigue • Jumpiness • Sweating • Difficulty sleeping • Rapid heartbeat • Dizziness • Nausea, vomiting or diarrhea • Frequent urination • Slow reaction times • Dry mouth • Muscular tension	• Anxiety • Grief • Inability to concentrate • Nightmares • Self doubt • Anger • Excessive concern with minor issues • Loss of confidence in self and unit	• Indecisiveness • Inattention • Carelessness • Hyper-alertness • Lack of motivation • Irritability • Lack of initiative • Tears, crying • Inability to relax • Argumentative

Severe Stress Reactions		
Physical	**Emotional**	**Behavioural**
• Constant movement • Severe startle response • Shaking or trembling • Weakness and paralysis • Impaired vision, hearing, and touch (loss of sensation) • Total exhaustion • Immobility • Stares vacantly • Acute abdominal pain • Impaired speech or muteness • Staggers or sways • Heart palpitations • Hyper ventilation • Insomnia/Severe sleep disturbance	• Anxiety • Grief • Inability to concentrate • Nightmares • Self doubt • Anger • Excessive concern with minor issues • Loss of confidence in self and unit	• Indecisiveness • Inattention • Carelessness • Hyper-alertness • Lack of motivation • Irritability • Lack of initiative • Tears, crying • Inability to relax • Argumentative

Appendix 3
Key terms in military psychiatry – from Department of Navy/US Marine Corps, Combat and Operational Stress Control (2010); NTTP 1-15M/MCRP 6-11C

adaptive coping – The normal, temporary process of coping with a stressor, usually by either changing oneself physically and mentally to be better suited for that particular stressor or by becoming numb to the mental and physical effects of that stressor. Stress adaptive coping is always temporary and it always fades after the stressor is no longer experienced.

combat and operational stress – The expected and predictable emotional, intellectual, physical, and/or behavioral reactions of Service members who have been exposed to stressful events in combat or noncombat military operations. Combat stress reactions vary in quality and severity as a function of operational conditions, such as intensity, duration, leadership, effective communication, unit morale, and perceived importance of the mission.

combat and operational stress control – Leader actions and responsibilities to promote resilience and psychological health in military units and individuals, including families, exposed to the stress of combat or other military operations.

combat and operational stress first aid – A set of tools with three simple aims: (1) preserve life, (2) prevent further harm, and (3) promote recovery. Combat and operational stress first aid components include the "seven Cs": check, coordinate, cover, calm, connect, competence, and confidence.

combat stress – Changes in physical or mental functioning or behavior resulting from the experience or lethal force or its aftermath. These changes can be positive and adaptive or they can be negative, including distress or loss of normal functioning.

operational stress – Changes in physical or mental functioning or behavior resulting from the experience or consequences of military operations other than combat, during peacetime or war, and on land, at sea, or in the air.

operational (or occupational) stress control – Leader actions and responsibilities to promote resilience and psychological health in military units and individuals, including family members, exposed to the stress of routine or wartime military operations in noncombat environments.

psychological first aid – Psychological support and assistance provided in the immediate aftermath of a traumatic event. Also called PFA.

stress illness – A diagnosable mental disorder resulting from an unhealed stress injury that worsens over time to cause significant disability in one or more spheres of life.

stress injury – More severe and persistent distress or loss of functioning caused by disruptions to the integrity of the brain, mind, or spirit after exposure to overwhelming stressors. Stress injuries are invisible but literal wounds caused by stress, but like more visible physical wounds, they usually heal, especially if given proper care.

stress reaction – The common, temporary, and often necessary experience of mild distress or changes in functioning due to stress from any cause.

Puzzle Answers
Word puzzle, page 76:
'The enemy is to the left flank.'

Intelligence test, pages 106–107:
Working from left to right, top to bottom, here are all the numbers for these boxes:

(total 15)	(total 27)	(total 39)
8 3 4	14 1 12	16 19 4
1 5 9	10 9 8	2 5 32
6 7 2	3 17 7	21 15 3

(total 18)	(total 24)	(total 60)
9 4 5	10 9 5	40 0 20
2 6 10	8 4 12	5 25 30
7 8 3	6 11 7	15 35 10

Index